Books in 1001 Questions Answered Series

Books in 1001 Questions Answered Series

1001 QUESTIONS ANSWERED ABOUT YOUR AQUARIUM
by Ida M. Mellen and Robert J. Lanier

1001 QUESTIONS ANSWERED ABOUT ASTRONOMY
by James S. Pickering

1001 QUESTIONS ANSWERED ABOUT BIRDS
by Allan D. Cruickshank and Helen G. Cruickshank

1001 QUESTIONS ANSWERED ABOUT BOATS AND BOATING
by ... R. de Kerchove and F. Devereux Joslin

1001 QUESTIONS ANSWERED ABOUT CHILD PSYCHOLOGY
by Andrew E. Shaw

1001 QUESTIONS ANSWERED ABOUT COOKING
by Charlotte Adams

1001 QUESTIONS ANSWERED ABOUT EARTH SCIENCE
by Richard M. Pearl

1001 QUESTIONS ANSWERED ABOUT FLOWERS
by N. Taylor

1001 QUESTIONS ANSWERED ABOUT INSECTS
by Alexander B. Klots and Elsie B. Klots

1001 QUESTIONS ANSWERED ABOUT THE MINERAL KINGDOM
by Richard M. Pearl

1001 QUESTIONS ANSWERED ABOUT THE NEW SCIENCE
by David O. Woodbury

1001 QUESTIONS ANSWERED ABOUT THE SEASHORE
by N. J. Berrill and Jacquelyn Berrill

1001 QUESTIONS ANSWERED ABOUT SPACE
by Gorton Carruth

1001 QUESTIONS ANSWERED ABOUT TREES
by Rutherford Platt

1001 QUESTIONS ANSWERED ABOUT THE WEATHER
by Frank H. Forrester

1001 Questions
Answered
About
Boats and
Boating

1001 Questions Answered About Boats and Boating

SSSSSSSSSSSSSSSSSSSSSS

BY W. H. DE FONTAINE AND B. DEVEREUX BARKER III

ILLUSTRATED WITH DRAWINGS

DODD, MEAD & COMPANY
NEW YORK

LIBRARY OF CONGRESS CATALOG CARD NUMBER: 66-14988

PRINTED IN THE UNITED STATES OF AMERICA

BY VAIL-BALLOU PRESS, INC., BINGHAMTON, N. Y.

To Dorothy and Mimi,
two sailors' wives

PREFACE

We heve attempted in this book to provide basic information on the several complex subjects which comprise the awareness of the complete yachtsman. Beginning with the selection of a suitable boat to meet the requirements for a particular situation, we take the reader through the various special fields of information, in capsule form, necessary to a well rounded knowledge of the subject.

It is our firm belief that the more one knows about a given sport the more pleasure he will derive from it. For that reason we have included in these pages the answers to the innumerable questions that are sure to occur to a boatman, be he a tyro or a more knowledgeable practitioner of the wonderful sport of yachting. Truly, in this book, he who runs may read, for we have striven to condense essential information into its most compact form. It is our hope that we may have contributed to the pleasure, knowledge, and safety of those who read these pages.

THE AUTHORS

CONTENTS

ILLUSTRATIONS

1001 Questions Answered About Boats and Boating

I. CHOOSING A BOAT

Introduction. The choice of a boat is a highly personal matter involving such consideration as your nautical experience, the size of your family, the size of your pocketbook, where you live, and also whether you prefer power boating or sailing, cruising, day sailing or racing. If you are young and your competitive spirit is highly developed, you will probably prefer racing, either power or sail. If you are older, the chances are that day sailing (and this includes power boating) or cruising will be your preference.

1. What is the simplest form of boat? The simplest boat, and the one in which a real beginner is likely to have his earliest experience, is a rowboat. These boats are propelled by oars and may be divided into several types such as flat bottom, V bottom, and round bottom. They also vary according to the shape of the bow, which may be pointed or "pram." A rowboat may also be driven by an outboard motor.

2. What is a pram? This is a rowboat whose bow (forward end) is square and has a "transom," like the stern (after or "back" end). Prams are usually shorter than boats with pointed bows.

3. How are prams used? They are mostly used as tenders for larger boats; yet some sailing prams are used by juniors to learn the rudiments of sailing.

4. How do rowing and sailing prams differ? A rowing pram is designed for propulsion by oars or an outboard motor. A sailing pram has a centerboard, a mast, a boom, a sail, and a rudder. A sailing pram can also be rowed.

5. What is a skiff? This is a form of rowboat, usually flat-bottomed, with a pointed bow. It can also be used with an outboard motor. A skiff can also be rigged for sailing, but this is not usual.

6. What is a dinghy? This is a term originally applied to a small boat intended for use as a tender to a larger boat. It may have a flat, V or round bottom and a pointed bow. It is a utility boat.

7. What is a sailing dinghy? This is a type of small sailboat that has been developed in this country since the 1920's. Some are utility dinghies, which are really yacht tenders that can be used for sailing, but there is a racing type that has been developed for sailing only. The latter type is divided into classes which are raced actively at many yacht clubs. The most popular classes vary from 9 feet to 11½ feet overall. Sail areas vary from 55 square feet to 72 square feet. All these boats are "cat-rigged." That is, they have only one sail. They are usually sailed with two people—one to sail, one for ballast.

8. How do you select a sailboat? After deciding about how much you want to invest in it, the first consideration is the kind of water in which you will be sailing. If your sailing area is shoal, you will need a centerboard. If the water is deep, a keelboat would also be practical. If there is a popular class in your area, you would be well advised to buy one of that type. When you get ready to sell you will find a better market.

9. Which type is most popular? The centerboard is the most popular as it can be sailed in shoal or deep water and is also easier to put on a trailer for transportation to different areas or to take home for winter storage. Small centerboarders are usually nonsinkable. They have proven faster than keelboats and usually cost less.

10. What are the disadvantages of small centerboarders? They can be capsized easier than a keelboat. The centerboard trunk bisects the cockpit and thus limits its space. The trunk sometimes develops leaks along its lower edge. In salt water it may be attacked on its inside surface by marine borers, so this area should be painted each season with antifouling paint. This requires removing the centerboard temporarily.

11. What are the advantages of keelboats? A well-designed keelboat should be noncapsizable. The absence of a centerboard trunk gives more space in the cockpit.

12. What are the disadvantages of a keelboat? Unless they are provided with adequate built-in flotation keelboats will sink if filled with water. They are also more difficult to load on a trailer or to haul out of water than a centerboard boat. A keelboat, being deeper, is more likely to run aground in shoal water. If it runs aground it is harder to get off again.

13. What is an International 14-footer? These are out and out racing machines. Their hulls are round-bottom and are just as light as they can be built. They carry a sloop rig (jib and mainsail) and are very fast and sporty boats to sail. But they are only for advanced sailors. They are never rowed. The usual crew is two people—one to steer and tend the mainsheet, the other to tend the jib sheet and the centerboard and to provide ballast.

14. What other small sailing classes are there? There are so many classes that to list them all is practically impossible, but they have certain things in common. Mostly, they are sloop-rigged centerboarders and carry a two-man crew. They range in size from about 10 feet to 19 feet overall.

15. What are some of the most popular centerboard sailing classes? Dyer Dhow (10 feet), Moth (11 feet), Penguin (11 feet 6 inches), Blue Jay (13 feet), Rhodes Bantam (14 feet), Snipe (15 feet 6 inches), Comet (16 feet), Thistle (17 feet), Rhodes 18 (18 feet), Lightning (19 feet). The first three are cat-rigged, the rest are sloops. The Moth is a one-man boat; the rest race with two aboard and sometimes the larger boats carry three.

16. What are some of the most popular keelboats? The Bull's-eye (16 feet) is a popular class along the eastern seaboard. The 110 (24 feet), 210 (29 feet) and Lightning (19 feet) are also popular in that area. The Star (22 feet) is a truly international class. These boats are owned and raced in almost every civilized country, and there are annual world championship races, as well as local and regional competition. Stars are frequently hauled to regattas on special trailers.

17. What is a scow? On our midwestern lakes and on Barnegat Bay bilgeboard scows are popular. They range in size from about 18 to 35 feet overall. The smaller are cat-rigged, the larger are sloops. They are very lightly built, decked hulls with twin rudders to agree with their bilgeboards. They have rounded bows and square sterns. Scows are highly developed, very fast racing machines and are not suitable for beginners. Most are of wood construction, but some of the smaller sizes are coming out with fiber-glass hulls.

18. What is a catamaran?   A new development in recent years is the catamaran. This type of boat has two hulls with space between and is very fast under favorable conditions. In primitive form they have been used for centuries by native boatmen in the South Sea islands and in South America. Modern catamarans are mostly small boats, ranging from 12 to 24 feet overall, and are primarily racing machines. However, larger ones have been built for cruising, and some have made long sea voyages. Some power-driven catamarans also have been built.

Although sailing catamarans have great initial stability they can be capsized. They also sometimes "pitchpole"—that is, they put their bows underwater when running before the wind, which can cause them to flip over forward. Generally speaking, the sailing of catamarans—at least in strong winds—had best be left to experts.

19. What is a trimaran?   This is a fast boat with three hulls. The center hull is the main one on which the crew rides. The two outside hulls are only to provide stability—that is, to keep the boat from capsizing. Some fairly large trimarans have been built, and at least one has crossed the Atlantic Ocean.

Trimarans have made fast times in several West Coast races and their use is spreading. Boats over 50 feet overall have been built, some for use as charter yachts—that is, they carry paying guests.

The type is popular in many foreign countries as well as the United States.

20. How are sailing yachts designated?   There are many ways to describe a yacht. Mostly it is her rig that distinguishes her. For example, she may be called a cat, a sloop, a cutter, yawl, ketch, or schooner. These six rigs are the ones most often used, but there are modifications according to the shape of the sails—gaff-headed or jib-headed, for example. In other words, a yacht might be referred to as jib-headed or gaff-headed plus the type of her rig—i.e., a jib-headed yawl or a gaff-headed schooner.

A further distinction can be used according to the shape of the yacht's bow—for example, a clipper-bowed, jib-headed yawl; a spoon-bowed, gaff-headed sloop; a clipper-bowed, staysail schooner; or a plumb-stemmed cat.

21. What is a catboat? The catboat is a single-masted vessel with the mast right up forward at the bow and a single sail.

Traditionally the catboat is a beamy centerboarder with a very large cockpit and a small cabin. Usually it has a big rudder hung over the stern which is sometimes called a barn door rudder.

The original catboats were gaff-rigged, but some modern cats have a jib-headed sail. While essentially similar, there are certain differences in local types of catboat which are distinguished by the names of the regions in which they were developed. For example the Cape Cod cat, the South Bay and the Barnegat cats. The first is a distinct type, native to the south shore of Cape Cod, many of which were built at Osterville, Massachusetts, by the Crosby family. These are also referred to as Crosby cats. The South Bay cat is native to Long Island's Great South Bay, and the typical boat differs in many respects from the Cape Cod type. Many were built by Gil Smith, a well-known designer-builder in the 1890's and early 1900's. They were lower sided than the Cape Codders, usually had overhangs fore and aft, and some had their masts further aft. And they were much faster.

Barnegat Bay (New Jersey) cats tend to have some of the characteristics of both the foregoing types.

In early days, Cape Cod cats were built as big as 50 feet overall and went offshore fishing, but most cats range from 30 feet overall down to 14 feet.

Sailing dinghies are technically catboats because they carry a cat rig; but their hulls are quite different from the traditional cat, and consequently they are not referred to as catboats.

22. What is a sloop? This is a single-masted vessel with the mast farther aft than a catboat's, and it carries both a mainsail and a jib. Big sloops sometimes carried two headsails—jib and staysail—but because the mast was well forward a sloop often had a bowsprit.

23. How does a cutter differ from a sloop?   The essential differences are the location of the mast and the fact that a true cutter usually has two headsails. The cutter, like the sloop, is a single-masted vessel, but the mast is located almost amidships (traditionally, 40 percent of the load waterline length from the forward end of the load waterline).

Some cutters have bowsprits and some are knockabouts. The terms "cutter" and "sloop" are used somewhat indiscriminately, except by purists.

24. What is an English cutter?   The original cutter was developed by the British. It was a deep-draft, narrow-beam vessel with a plumb stern, a long bowsprit, a fidded topmast over the mainmast, and carried a jib, staysail, mainsail, and topsail. A jib topsail could also be set on the topmast stay. Yachts of this type are referred to as English cutters but are seldom seen anymore.

25. What is a yawl?   This is a two-masted vessel with the mainmast forward (like a sloop) and a smaller mast, called a mizzenmast (or jigger), stepped abaft the after end of the load waterline. A yawl may be rigged with either jib-headed or gaff-headed sails. Or she may carry one of each.

The headsails of a yawl are similar to those of a sloop, ketch, or schooner.

26. What is a ketch?   The principal difference between a yawl and a ketch lies in the position of the mizzenmast, which is forward of the after end of the load waterline on a ketch. And the mizzen sail is larger than that of a yawl in relation to the mainsail. Conversely, the mainsail of a ketch is proportionately smaller than that of a yawl of the same size. The headsails of both yawl and ketch are similar.

27. How do you recognize a schooner?   Most schooner yachts are two-masted vessels whose masts are the same height, or the mainmast, which is the aftermost spar, is the taller. There are a few three-masted schooner yachts. Schooners may be of several rigs, but they usually carry a double head rig—jib and staysail. The sail that is carried on the foremast is called the foresail, and it is generally gaff-headed. The mainsail is carried on the mainmast and may be either gaff- or jib-headed.

Gaff-headed schooners often carry a topsail over the main.

Many schooners carry a sail between the masts, called a fisherman staysail. It is a four-sided sail filling the space from main masthead or main topmast head to fore masthead, extending partway down the foremast, and trims aft, like a jib.

28. What is a staysail schooner?   This is a schooner (usually two-masted) that carries a jib-headed mainsail but no gaff-foresail. Instead it carries a main staysail rigged just like a foresail. Over this it usually carries a fisherman staysail, but a few staysail schooners have been rigged with wishbone foresails instead of a fisherman staysail.

The headsail arrangement is conventional.

29. What is a knockabout?   This term is applied to a boat with headsails, but without a bowsprit.

30. What is a Marconi rig?   This is a misnomer for a jib-headed rig. Originally used in England, the term "Marconi" described a very tall, one-piece mast which was elaborately stayed, like early wooden wireless masts. The term was applied also to the sail, which is improperly referred to as a Marconi sail or Marconi rig. Actually the inventor of wireless communication had nothing to do with developing this rig.

31. What is a jib-headed sail?   This is a term used to describe a sail hoisted on a mast by a single halyard, like a jib. It is three-cornered and its parts bear the same designations as those of a jib.

It takes the name of the mast on which it is carried—i.e., jib-headed mainsail, jib-headed mizzen, etc.

Jib-headed sails are sometimes miscalled Marconi sails. The British also call them Bermudian.

32. What is a gunter rig?   At first glance this looks like a jib-headed sail, but actually it is a gaff-headed sail whose gaff is hoisted close to the after side of the mast. It is not much used in the United States, but is popular in England, mostly on sailing dinghies.

The mast is shorter than with a true jib-headed rig, and a single

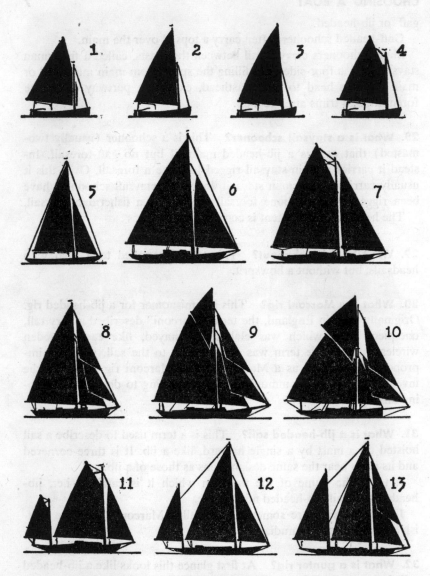

KINDS OF RIGS

(1) Standing Lug cat; (2) Sliding Gunter cat; (3) Jib-headed (Marconi) cat; (4) Gaff-headed cat; (5) Jib-headed sloop (knockabout rig); (6) Jib-headed sloop; (7) Gaff-headed sloop; (8) Jib-headed cutter; (9) Gaff-headed cutter; (10) English cutter; (11) Gaff-headed yawl; (12) Jib-headed yawl; (13) Jib-headed ketch

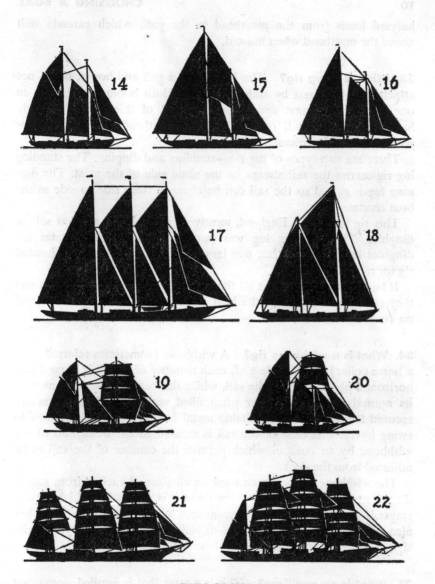

KINDS OF RIGS

(14) Gaff-headed, two-masted schooner; (15) Staysail rigged, two-masted schooner; (16) Jib-headed main, gaff-headed fore schooner; (17) Three-masted staysail schooner; (18) Staysail (wishbone) ketch; (19) Brigantine (formerly called Hermaphrodite Brig); (20) Topsail schooner; (21) Ship; (22) Four-masted bark

halyard leads from the masthead to the gaff, which extends well above the masthead when hoisted.

33. What is a lug rig?   The lugsail has a gaff and boom, but is not attached to the mast by slides or hoops. Both boom and gaff lie to one side of the mast and extend forward of it slightly. A single halyard hoists the gaff (or yard) to the masthead, and the boom is secured with a downhaul.

There are two types of lug rig—standing and dipping. The standing lug rig carries the sail always on the same side of the mast. The dipping lug is rigged so the sail can be changed from side to side as the boat changes tacks.

This rig is used in England, mostly on small boats such as sailing dinghies. The standing lug was popular in the United States for dinghies in the 1930's, but was largely superseded by the jib-headed rig for racing.

It has the advantage that all three spars can be the same length and they can be stowed inside the boat when it is being towed or carried on deck.

34. What is a wishbone rig?   A wishbone (sometimes referred to as a horse collar) is a double gaff, each member of which is curved in a horizontal plane to allow the sail, which lies between them, to assume its normal shape or camber when filled with wind. Wishbones are secured to the mast with suitable metal fittings which allow them to swing freely. The clew of the sail is secured to the outer end of the wishbone by an outhaul which permits the camber of the sail to be adjusted from the deck.

The wishbone rig has been used on all sizes of yachts, from sailing dinghies to big ocean racers. Sometimes it is used with a high-clewed staysail, sometimes with a conventional jib-headed mainsail. It has also been used in place of a fore-staysail boom, mostly on yachts designed by Frederick Fenger, of Cohasset, Massachusetts.

35. What is an auxiliary?   This is a term that is applied, somewhat loosely, both to a sailboat's engine and to the boat itself. One refers to a sailboat that has an engine as an auxiliary sloop, an auxiliary yawl, etc. Or one can say that a sailboat has an auxiliary engine.

36. What is a "goldplater"? This is a slang term used to describe an expensive, extra well equipped and highly finished yacht.

37. What is a cruising sailboat? A cruising sailboat is anywhere from 20 feet in overall length (sometimes even less) and up. It has interior accommodations, and may be lived aboard for an extended period of time. It is also normally powered by an auxiliary engine and may carry any rig.

38. What is an ocean racer? An ocean racer is a cruising sailboat that is equipped and manned to race at sea for extended periods of time. Special safety equipment is generally required by the organization sponsoring a race. It may carry any sailing rig, but the most popular are sloops, cutters, yawls, and ketches. In the past the schooner rig was popular for ocean racing, but now few yachts with this rig race seriously.

39. What is an auxiliary engine? An auxiliary engine in a sailboat is a mechanical secondary source of propulsion that is used when sailing is not possible or advisable (as in getting in and out of harbors).
  Engines used to drive electric generators, bilge pumps, capstans, or other mechanical gear are also referred to as auxiliaries.

40. What is the meaning of the term "flush deck"? A flush deck boat has very little or no superstructure above deck level. Boats of this type use skylights to let light below and are normally higher-sided to provide the necessary headroom in the cabin.

41. What is a powerboat? A powerboat (or motorboat) has as its primary source of propulsion an engine or engines. If it has sail, it is used for steadying purposes only, or in an emergency.

42. What is a motor sailer? A motor sailer is a cruising yacht that is equally effective under either power or sail. The hull design will normally incorporate features of both types. Its engine (or engines) will be much more powerful than that of a comparable auxiliary sailboat, while the area of its sailing rig will usually be somewhat smaller.

43. What is a hydroplane? A hydroplane is the fastest of all racing powerboats. It normally has two planing surfaces forward, called sponsons, and one aft. At high speeds hydroplane hulls become completely airborne with only the bottom part of the propeller remaining in the water.

Unlimited Class hydroplanes of the type that race for the Gold Cup have reached speeds in excess of 200 m.p.h. These are sometimes called gold cuppers (not to be confused with goldplaters, which see).

44. What is a hydrofoil boat? A hydrofoil has pontoon-like planes or foils on which the boat rides when it rises out of the water after attaining the necessary speed. The foils are attached beneath the hull with struts which support the boat clear of the water. Such boats can attain great speed and are relatively free of motion caused by waves. Large hydrofoils arc used in many countries (mostly in Europe) to carry passengers for short distances.

45. What is a "hovercraft" or an air-cushion boat? This is a new type of craft which can operate over land or water and is supported slightly above the surface on a cushion of air provided by a suitable power plant which forces air in a downward direction, providing an air cushion on which the craft floats.

46. What is an inboard powerboat? This is one with its engine installed permanently within the hull.

47. How are pleasure powerboats classified? First, by propulsion, as inboards, outboards, or outdrives. Second, by purpose, as runabouts, cruisers, utilities, or racing boats.

Commercial craft are not discussed here.

48. What is an outboard powerboat? This is a boat that is driven by an outboard engine.

49. What is an outdrive boat? This is a boat that is driven by an outdrive (inboard/outboard) power unit.

50. What is an outdrive (inboard/outboard) power unit? This is a new concept in powerboat propulsion in which the power is supplied by a conventional inboard engine permanently installed at the boat's stern and connected to a drive unit which is bolted to the boat's transom. This unit has certain characteristics in common with an outboard engine: It can be tipped up to avoid obstructions, for mooring in shoal water or for carrying on a trailer. It also turns from side to side, so it serves as a rudder to steer the boat, as does an outboard motor.

51. What are the advantages of outdrive over an inboard engine installation? The engine is located away aft, out of the way, no propeller shaft or stuffing box is required, thus reducing possible leaks, and no rudder is used. The unit can be retracted as needed.

52. What are the advantages of in outdrive unit over an outboard motor? Its construction is more rugged; engines of greater power are available; and if the engine is a four-cycle one, much less fuel is consumed. Also, there is little or no chance that it will be stolen, as outboard engines frequently are.

II. PURCHASING AND COSTS

Introduction. There are several ways of going about buying a boat. In most boating communities there are yacht brokers who maintain listings of used boats for sale, and some also act as dealers for new boats. If advice is needed as to the most suitable boat to buy, one can usually depend on the recommendations of a reputable broker. If a used boat is purchased through a broker, his fee is paid by the seller.

Local newspapers and national boating magazines carry a great deal of brokerage advertising that will help in locating a particular type of boat. Boats are also sold directly by owners through classified advertising in these publications.

A very complete listing of the products of practically every United States boatbuilder (and some foreign builders) is to be found in the *Boat Owners Buyers Guide,* published by Yachting Publishing Corporation, 50 West 44th Street, New York, New York 10036.

53. Must one first own a boat in order to learn the sport? No. There are many other possibilities as you will gather as you read along.

54. Does one have to belong to a yacht club to get started in or learn about boating? No. In most areas there are public facilities and in some places local governments even sponsor boating classes. Sailing schools, summer camps, and a few boys' prep schools offer classes in sailing. Consult the advertising pages of boating magazines and the yellow pages of the telephone directory.

55. What national organizations offer the public free instruction in all aspects of boating? The United States Power Squadron, whose headquarters are located in Englewood, New Jersey. This organization has more than 69,000 members and has branches throughout the country. These can usually be found in local telephone books.

The U.S. Coast Guard Auxiliary also offers free instruction courses to the public. The Auxiliary is organized into seventeen district headquarters that cover the entire country. A listing of classes may be had from the district director in your area. See your local phone book.

56. Do some boat dealers have sailing instruction programs? Yes, a list of those in your local area that do is maintained by the American Sailing Council, a division of the National Association of Engine and Boat Manufacturers, 420 Lexington Avenue, New York, New York 10017.

57. How does one go about joining a yacht club? As with most clubs, one must be proposed and seconded by members of the club. The admissions committee then acts upon the membership proposal. There are, however, some commercial yacht clubs which require only the payment of a fee in order to join.

58. How much do new boats cost? At the lower end of the price bracket is the flat-bottom skiff which can be bought new for $100 to $200. Most small sailing dinghies are in the $500 range. When you get into the 12- to 20 foot classes, figure from $50 to $125 per foot overall. This refers only to day sailing and racing boats. Those with cruising accommodations will come much higher. Well-built modern yachts with cruising accommodations will cost from $750 to $2,000 per foot of overall length, depending on quality and equipment.

59. How much does it cost to operate a boat? This is a difficult question to answer, as so much depends on the type of boat and the amount of maintenance done by her owner. A boat that can be hauled home on a trailer for the winter and is put in commission in the spring by her owner is the most economical. On the other hand, if she is stored in a boatyard which does all the commissioning, it will cost a good deal for her yearly operation.

Sailboats, because they consume no fuel, cost less to operate than powerboats. Some of the costs of operation are depreciation, maintenance, insurance, personal property taxes (in some localities), club dues or marina charges, fuel (for powerboats and auxiliaries), plus miscellaneous expenses. As a rule of thumb it will cost from 20 to 25 percent of a boat's original cost to operate her for a year, if she is stored in a boatyard. Cost of operation is related to a boat's displacement (weight). The heavier the boat, the greater the cost.

A cost factor usually overlooked is the loss of income on the amount of money invested in the boat. In the case of a $5,000 boat, for example, if the money were in a savings bank at 4 percent interest, the annual return would be $200. The cash return from the same investment in a boat is nil.

60. What are the four possibilities for berthing a boat? You can keep her on a trailer, rent a mooring or marina slip, or join a club with waterfront facilities. If you own waterfront property it should be no problem.

61. How much do used boats cost? A used boat in good condition will probably cost two-thirds to three-quarters as much as a new one. If the price asked is low, there may be some fault with the boat, and it should be carefully surveyed before purchase.

It is wise to have any used boat surveyed before purchase.

62. How can a prospective owner have a boat surveyed before purchase? Normally a yacht broker or local boatyard can recommend a naval architect or other boating expert who engages in this work professionally for a fee. As in any profession, an individual's reputation is best known by those who deal with him every day.

63. What other fees (besides the surveyor's) may a new boat owner expect to encounter in purchasing a boat? There is a small fee in most states today for registering a boat with an engine of ten horsepower or more. Registration is required by federal law, and where states have not enacted their own laws, registration is handled by the U.S. Coast Guard or similar government agency.

64. What fee will a broker normally charge in selling a boat? A yacht broker makes no charge for listing a boat for sale. His only fee comes when the boat is actually sold, and he then collects an amount in the neighborhood of 5 percent or more of the value of the vessel. This fee is paid by the individual selling the boat. The amount of the fee usually varies according to the size and cost of the boat involved; the greater the amount involved, the smaller the percentage of the fee.

65. Can it be generally established what the worth of a particular type or size of boat will be at a given age? Yes, the stock outboards and cruisers and one-design classes have a regional value that is listed in a directory similar to the book used by automobile dealers.

In addition the condition and equipment, such as sails, will have a bearing on the value.

Such a used boat directory is published by Boats Unlimited Corporation, 2005 Palmer Avenue, Larchmont, New York.

66. What determines the depreciation of a standard model boat? There appears to be no set pattern. Boats of different manufacturers, and even different models of the same manufacturer, depreciate at varying rates. Current economic conditions throughout the country will, of course, have substantial effect.

67. Is it possible to buy a boat on an installment basis? Yes, boat dealers will offer installment buying just as automobile dealers do. Banks will often finance the purchase of a boat up to 75 percent of its cost.

68. Is it less expensive to build a large boat abroad? In many cases yes, primarily because labor is often cheaper. There is an import duty, 7.5 percent and up, which is substantially less if the boat is used, but it is not enough to make up the difference in any case.

69. Why do boats of fiber-glass construction often cost somewhat less than boats of other materials? Because boats of fiber-glass are mass produced from the same molds with very little preparation necessary in between.

70. What is the meaning of the term "fully found" with respect to a boat available for sale or charter? A fully found boat is completely seaworthy and equipped with everything required for normal use.

71. What annual publication contains complete listings of all known manufacturers of boats, engines, and equipment of all kinds? The *Boat Owners Buyers Guide* is just such a volume. It is available by sending $1.50 to BOBG, 50 West 44th Street, New York, New York 10036.

72. What are the national boating trade associations? The National Association of Engine and Boat Manufacturers, located in New York, and the Outboard Boating Club of America, located in

Chicago.

The NAEBM sponsors the annual National Boat Show in New York during January.

73. What is chartering?   Chartering a boat is, in many respects, like renting a house, except that the term may vary from an hour or two to a season or years. And the point of delivery can usually be arranged to suit the charterer.

74. How do you charter a boat?   Usually through a yacht broker who maintains lists of boats that are available. But occasionally a charter can be arranged directly with an owner.

75. What advantages does chartering (versus owning) offer? Chartering offers many advantages. For example, no capital investment is required, and overall operating costs such as maintenance, depreciation, and insurance are paid by the owner. The charterer has a wide choice of the type of boat he may want at the time—sloop, yawl, ketch, etc., or a powerboat.

Another advantage is that the boat can usually be taken over in the area where it will be used.

76. What costs are assumed by the charter party?   Only the cost of operating the boat while under charter: fuel, food, dockage or mooring fees, etc., which are sometimes included in the basic charter fee.

III. LEARNING TO SAIL

Introduction. Learning to handle a boat under sail is not a difficult task once the fundamentals have been grasped. A feel for sailing comes more easily to some people than to others, and it is difficult to predict in advance how long it will take a particular individual to develop his skills. Experience and practice are the best teachers once the essentials are learned and a certain degree of confidence attained.

It is best, of course, to start sailing at an early age. The top sailors are almost always those who have been at it all their lives. This does not mean, however, that an adult cannot start sailing and become proficient in time. Some of the people who enjoy sailing most are those who became interested in it as adults.

One noticeable trend in the United States in recent years has been a movement of outboard runabout owners into small sailboats. This is probably because as they learn more about the water they look for more of a challenge—and learning to sail offers that.

77. At what age can sailing be taught? As soon as a youngster is able to swim fifty yards it may be considered safe for him to sail alone in a patrolled area. However, many children have learned to sail wearing life jackets and with adults aboard at a very young age—say six or seven years old. Most junior instruction programs do not take children until they are eight or nine years old.

78. What should be the prime objective of a junior sailing program? A junior program should first of all impart a love and respect for the sea and its traditions. Then it should produce competent sailors to fill out the ranks of future yachtsmen.

79. In sailing, what is meant by the term "junior yachtsman"? By definition of the North American Yacht Racing Union, a junior has not reached his eighteenth birthday by September 1 of a given year.

80. What is the proper procedure in hoisting sails? Always hoist the aftermost sail first and proceed forward. Only hoist headsails after the mooring is dropped or the anchor is weighed.

81. What is the proper procedure when lowering sails? Begin with headsails and proceed toward the stern, lowering the aftermost sail last.

82. Why are sails hoisted and lowered as previously described? To prevent the boat from sailing about her anchor or mooring. One must remember that he is dealing with two forces or pressures when making (hoisting) or lowering sail.

The pressure of water is acting on a fixed point—the center of lateral resistance (CLR) of the hull and appendages (rudder, centerboard) as the pivot point acts on a weathervane.

Wind pressure is exerted on the center of effort (CE) of the sails. The further aft the CE, the more the boat (and weathervane) tends to head into the wind.

The CLR of keelboats is a fixed point, but on a centerboarder it can be modified somewhat by adjusting the position of the board. The CE of the sail plan is susceptible to quick and radical adjustment. If, when a boat is lying to an anchor, her headsails alone should be hoisted, she would horse around out of control. On the other hand, if her aftermost sail is hoisted first, and the sheet trimmed, she will lie quietly, head to wind. Remember the weathervane.

83. What is done with the sails after a mooring is picked up and secured? Lower all headsails at once to keep the boat from sailing about at her mooring. On a sloop, cutter, or schooner the mainsail is the last to come down. On a yawl or ketch it is the second sail to be lowered (assuming a single headsail), the mizzen being left standing until last.

84. How is wind direction designated? It is the point of the compass from which a wind is blowing that determines what it is called. For example, a wind coming from the east is called an east wind.

85. What is meant by apparent wind? For the sailor there can be two wind directions at the same time—true and apparent. When a boat is stationary, as at anchor, the only wind that affects it is the true wind. And this is also true if the boat is moving directly toward or away from the true wind's direction.

But when a boat moves at an angle to the direction of the true wind, it sets up a wind of its own whose direction depends on the boat's speed. Perhaps the best illustration of this phenomenon is the flag on the bow staff of a powerboat. Assume the true wind is west at 10 knots and that the boat is headed south at the same speed. It is moving at 90 degreees to the true wind's direction, and the flag (being affected equally by the forces of the true wind and that set up by the boat's forward movement) will fly at an angle of 45 degrees to the boat's center line. The apparent wind indicated by the flag would be SW. If it were a calm day the flag (being affected only by the boat's own movement) would fly straight aft.

86. Why is the direction of the apparent wind important to a sailor? Because it is the wind by which he must sail his boat. And every boat has its own private apparent wind. The faster the boat, the farther ahead the apparent wind will be. With the true wind abeam at 10 knots, a 5-knot boat could probably carry a spinnaker, but a faster boat's apparent wind would be so far ahead that she could not carry a spinnaker to advantage.

This is the reason that a catamaran can't point as close as a displacement boat. A good catamaran sails so much faster than conventional boats that its apparent wind comes farther ahead.

87. What are the six points of sailing? They are close hauled, full-and-by, close reach, beam reach, broad reach, and run.

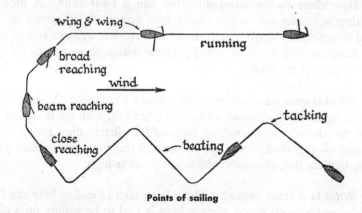

Points of sailing

88. When is a boat close-hauled?   When her sheets are trimmed as far in as they can be and she is heading as close as she can sail to the wind a boat is said to be close-hauled, hard on the wind, or sailing dead to windward. On this point of sailing the leading edges or luffs of her sails will be just aflutter.

89. What is meant by sailing to windward?   Sailing to windward is the same as sailing close-hauled. You are trying to reach an objective that is dead into the wind, and you must tack to get there.

The idea is to sail as close to the wind as possible and still maintain reasonable speed through the water.

90. What is meant by the expression "hard on the wind?"   This is a term used to describe the condition of a sailing yacht when she is sailing as close to the wind as possible. In other words, the sheets are trimmed in hard and she is going to windward to the best of her ability. This is the same as "close-hauled."

91. What is meant by the term "pointing"?   When sailing to windward, a boat is said to point well if she sails particularly close to the wind.

92. What is meant when a boat is said to be footing?   To foot is to bear off slightly when sailing to windward in order to gain greater speed. To foot faster is to make more speed.

93. How close to the wind direction can a boat sail?   A modern cruising boat can sail within about four points (45 degrees) of the wind direction. A highly tuned racing boat with a well-cut suit of sails can head somewhat closer, some perhaps within three points (almost 34 degrees) of the wind.

94. What is meant by full-and-by?   When a boat that is sailing close-hauled bears off slightly so all her sails are full, with no flutter at the luffs, she is said to be sailing full-and-by. Sheets may be eased or slacked off slightly and she will go through the water faster than when close-hauled. But, of course, she won't point as high.

95. What is a close reach?   There is an area of sailing between full-and-by and a beam reach when a boat is said to be sailing on a close reach. Sheets are eased more than when full-and-by and more speed is attained. This is in fact one of the fastest points of sailing. The apparent wind is forward of the beam.

96. What is a beam reach?   When anything is broadside to a boat it is said to be abeam. Hence a beam reach is the point of sailing when the apparent wind is at 90 degrees to a boat's course. Sheets are trimmed so booms are about 45 degrees from the center line of the boat. The apparent wind is said to be abeam.

97. What is a broad reach?   The area of sailing between a beam reach and a run is called a broad reach. Sheets are eased until booms are at almost 90 degrees to the wind, as the boat's head is turned farther from the wind's direction. The apparent wind is aft of amidships.

98. When is a boat running?   When the wind (both true and apparent) is coming from astern, a boat is said to be running before the wind. Her sheets will be as far off as they can be trimmed without spillng wind from the sails.

99. What is meant by tacking?   To tack is to alter course when close-hauled to cross the direction from which the wind is coming so that it will come from the other side of the boat. The boat comes head to wind during this maneuver.

100. What is the meaning of the expression "coming about"?   This is the same as tacking—going from one tack to the other.

101. How are the two tacks designated?   A boat is said to be on starboard tack if the direction from which the wind is coming is over the starboard (right side looking forward) rail. A boat is on port tack if the wind is coming over the port (left) side.

102. How is the main boom adjusted when tacking?   In beating to windward, it is not necessary to adjust the trim of the main boom. It will come over to the new tack by itself and need not be touched.

103. What is a jibe?   A jibe is the opposite of a tack. When sailing before the wind, a yacht jibes when her course is changed so the boom moves from the side on which it had been carried to the side opposite.

104. How is the main boom jibed?   Just before the helm is put over to change course, the main boom should be trimmed amidships. It is then allowed to run out on the new tack as the course changes. The boom should never be allowed to jibe over by itself. In the distance it travels a boom can build up considerable speed in a strong wind and can cause damage if allowed to jibe unchecked.

105. How is a spinnaker jibe accomplished?   The spinnaker pole is moved from one clew of the sail to the other at the same time that the sheet and guy are adjusted for the new heading.

106. What are the two principal ways of jibing a spinnaker?   The "dipping" method is used on most larger boats. With this system the inboard end of the spinnaker pole is raised high enough on the mast so that the outboard end, when lowered, will swing under the head-stay.

In the "end-for-end" system, used on smaller boats, the pole is detached from the mast, and the points of attachment at the sail and at the mast are reversed.

107. What makes a sailboat go to windward?   Three forces operate to cause a boat to go to windward: the pressure of the water on the leeward side of the hull (lateral resistance), the pressure of the wind on the windward side of her sails, and the partial vacuum that develops on the leeward side of her sails. The combination of these is what causes a boat to go to windward.

108. What are the relative proportions of pressure and vacuum on the sails of a boat going to windward?   Wind tunnel experiments have pretty conclusively shown that the forward drive imparted to the sails of a boat hard on the wind is divided about 20–40 percent pressure on the windward side and 60–80 percent vacuum on the leeward side. The vacuum can be increased with a suitable overlapping jib, causing what is called a slot effect.

109. What is meant by the slot effect?   This is the increased vacuum
developed on the lee side of a sail when a jib or staysail ahead of it is
trimmed so as to cause the wind to accelerate in passing. This acceleration causes a drop in static pressure on the lee side of the sail, with
the result that it tends to move in the direction of the partial vacuum,
thus causing the boat to sail faster.

Slot effect is based on the Venturi principle.

110. What sail causes the greatest slot effect?   A big overlapping
Genoa jib has been found to produce the greatest forward drive in a
boat sailing close-hauled (hard on the wind). It overlaps the mainsail
and parallels it to leeward, forming a slot and forcing the wind
trapped between the sails to speed up in passing.

111. How can one demonstrate slot effect?   Hold a flat sheet of letter paper at two corners; place its edge just below your lower lip and
blow over its upper surface. The resulting acceleration of air causes a
decrease in static pressure on the upper surface. As the static pressure
on the lower surface remains unchanged, the difference in pressures
will cause the paper to rise to a horizontal position. This illustrates
one of the forces that causes boats to sail.

**112. How can one tell when a boat is properly balanced going to
windward?**   In an average breeze, 10 to 12 knots, a boat that is
properly balanced should have a slight weather helm.

113. What is meant by weather helm?   Weather helm occurs when
the rudder of a sailboat must be used to keep her from heading up
into the wind. A little weather helm is desirable when sailing to windward, as it helps to keep a boat headed as close to wind as possible
yet still maintaining speed. The proper amount of weather helm also
gives a boat "feel," a slight tug on the helm (tiller or wheel) letting
the helmsman know she is there.

114. What is lee helm?   Lee helm is the opposite of weather
helm. The boat with lee helm has a tendency to bear off when sailing
close-hauled, which is not considered desirable.

115. What is a good general rule on how hard a Genoa should be trimmed? A Genoa jib should never be trimmed so hard that it touches a spreader.

116. How can you tell quickly if any sail is properly trimmed? Generally speaking, a sail is properly trimmed when its leading edge (luff) is just on the point of breaking or luffing (fluttering).

117. What causes a sail to luff? A sail is caused to luff when equalized wind pressure exists on both of its sides. This always occurs first at a sail's leading edge when a boat is headed into the wind.

118. When is it desirable to have a flat mainsail? In heavy breezes a flat sail will keep its drive a great deal longer and be more effective than a full-cut one. This is particularly true on boats with large Genoa jibs which backwind mainsails to a considerable degree.

119. What is a boom vang? This is a tackle used to keep a boom that is mounted on a mast (as distinguished from one on a staysail) from lifting due to wind pressure in the sail. Leading from the lowest practical position on the mast (or the leeward rail) to a point on the boom about 25 percent of its length from the mast, a vang exerts downward pressure on the boom and thus helps to keep the sail flat.

120. Is a boom vang useful in windward sailing? Yes. A boom vang is of considerable advantage in controlling the draft of a mainsail. This device is also called a kicking strap in England.

121. How do good racing sailors hold a tiller? Top racing skippers generally advise holding a tiller as lightly as possible to reduce unnecessary movement to a minimum and to gain as much "feel" as possible. Normally just the thumb and first two fingers are enough to control the tiller of a well-balanced small boat. Larger boats will require more effort.

122. What is a tiller extension? Tiller extensions are used on small boats where it is desirable for the skipper to hike out. They are attached to the tiller end so that they can swing in any direction to be used most effectively by the helmsman who is a good distance away. They are also called hiking sticks.

123. What is meant by hiking out? This is a term applied to the act of placing one's weight as far to windward as possible in order to offset the tendency of a sailboat to heel under the pressure of wind in her sails.

124. How should one move about a sailboat? Cautiously and gently. Violent movements have a bad effect on a boat's balance and generally tend to decrease her speed.

125. What is backwind? Backwind is the disturbed air caused by the sails of a boat in a cone-shaped area aft and to leeward. Such air is said to be foul.

A Genoa jib backwinds the mainsail on the same boat to some extent, causing it to luff.

126. When is a reef taken in a sail? A reef is taken in a sail to reduce the exposed area of the sail, due to increased velocity of the wind and to other sea conditions. This point will vary on each boat according to her sail-carrying ability.

127. How is roller reefing accomplished? As the main halyard is slacked, the crank of the roller reefing gear is turned, which rolls the sail on the boom. It is usually necessary to spill the wind from the sail by easing the mainsheet or heading the boat into the wind. The reef will be neater if the leech of the sail is kept under tension while the boom rotates.

128. How is a conventional reef tied in? If under sail, the halyard is eased the desired amount. Reefing pendants are run through tack and clew cringles to form new lashings and secured. The portion of the sail to be reefed is then rolled tight by hand and tied with the reef points in bows or reef knots. Reef points do not go around the boom, merely around the bunt of the sail, except in cases where the sail's foot is in a slot.

Before the halyard is slacked off make sure the topping lift is adjusted so that the boom will not come crashing down as the halyard is eased.

The easiest way to tie in a reef is to do it before the sail is hoisted. Follow the procedure just outlined, except that the halyard is not touched until the reefed sail is ready for hoisting.

129. Can a boat be sailed backward? Yes. And this can be quite useful under some conditions—for example, if you want to set your anchor more securely or change your position at anchor to a place farther astern.

In such cases it is only necessary to slowly push the main boom—with sail set, of course—first to one side, then to the other. The boat will gather sternway slowly and can be backed for considerable distances.

This technique is also useful as a brake to slow down a boat's approach to a dock or mooring buoy.

As a stunt, a sailing dinghy or other small boat can be sailed backward by holding the boom broad off while steering with the rudder to offset the tendency to sail in circles.

130. Can a sailboat be handled without a rudder? Yes. By properly balancing and trimming the sails, boats can be, and have been, sailed great distances after losing their rudders. This is usually accomplished by a trial and error procedure, as proper sail balance on one boat can be quite different on another.

131. Can a boat be handled without a rudder on every point of sailing? Yes. By balancing and trimming one sail against another, a boat can be sailed in any direction that would normally be possible. It is easiest, however, if the boat without a rudder can be sailed reasonably close-hauled.

IV. SAILS, SPARS, AND RIGGING

Introduction. The above-deck equipment on any sailboat—consisting primarily of sails, spars, and rigging—determines to a large extent the degree of racing success that a boat will enjoy. A properly cut sail on a well-tuned mast is a sight to delight the sailor's eye. A rig that looks sloppy will probably perform poorly and be indicative of the type of seaman employing it. Here we will learn of the essential details that go into making the motive power of a sailboat perform as it should.

132. What is a mainsail?   As the name implies, this is the principle sail of a vessel.

133. What is a mizzen?   On a yawl or ketch, the mizzen is the small sail away aft, rigged to the mizzenmast.

134. What is a spinnaker?   The spinnaker is the parachute-like sail that a boat carries instead of a jib when sailing off the wind. It is common practice to carry this sail when racing even when the apparent wind is slightly forward of the beam.

135. What is the origin of the term "spinnaker"?   In 1886 the English sailmaking firm of Ratsey & Lapthorn cut an enormous light sail for the yacht *Sphinx,* which became known as the *"Sphinx*'s acre."* This gradually evolved into the word we know today as spinnaker.

136. What is a jib?   This is the sail carried before the mast of a sailboat. It is mounted on a wire stay with jib hanks or snap hooks. There are many kinds of jibs for use according to conditions.

137. What is a Genoa jib?   This is one of the most important sails on a racing yacht, filling the whole fore triangle and overlapping the mainsail for a large part of its area.

138. When is a Genoa jib carried?   This sail should be used only when the wind is forward of the beam. In fact it is most effective when a yacht is hard on the wind.

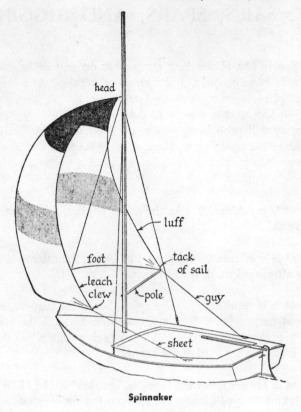

Spinnaker

139. How did the Genoa jib come by its name?   The first jib to be given the name was used aboard a Swedish six-meter yacht that was engaged in a series of races off the city of Genoa, on the Mediterranean Sea. The sail thereafter was, quite naturally, referred to by its owner, Sven Salen, as his Genoa jib.

140. Whose idea was the Genoa jib?   The Swedish yachtsman Sven Salen (rhymes with clean) is credited with having first conceived this sail for his six-meter yacht *Maybe* when he was engaged in a series of championship races off the city of Genoa in 1927.

141. What is a Swedish jib?   This was a name that, at one time, was applied to the sail now universally referred to as a Genoa jib. No doubt the reason for such a designation was because the sail was first used by the Swedish yachtsman Sven Salen.

142. What is a working jib? This is the sail that is carried under normal conditions. It is usually made of the same weight cloth as the mainsail.

143. What is a storm jib? This is a small sail of extra-strong cloth, which is used in heavy weather.

144. What is a jib topsail? This is a small jib that is carried on a stay leading from the topmast head to the end of the bowsprit or to the stemhead of a knockabout rig. It is a light-weather sail, not often seen in recent years.

145. What is a topsail? This is a triangular sail that is used only over gaff-headed sails. On schooners the topsails were called main-topsail or fore-topsail, depending on which mast they were hoisted on.

Topsails on big yachts were also classified as working or club, according to the way they were made. A working topsail was hoisted on a topmast, to which it was held by means of wooden hoops. Its clew led to the peak of the gaff, and the tack downhaul led down to the deck. When furled it was brailed up to the lower masthead by means of lines called brails. A crew member was sent aloft to put stops around the sail after it was brailed up.

The club topsail is also a triangular sail, but it differs from the working topsail by being larger and having two spars, a yard and a club, lashed to it. The yard goes against the topmast and the club against the gaff. These sails were used mostly on the main-topmasts of racing boats.

146. What is a foresail? This is the sail rigged on the leading, or fore, mast of a schooner.

147. What is a staysail? As the name implies, this sail is usually carried on a stay (like a jib). On larger boats, which may carry more than one headsail, the forestaysail is the one closest to the mast. Where there is only one headsail it is usually referred to as a jib.

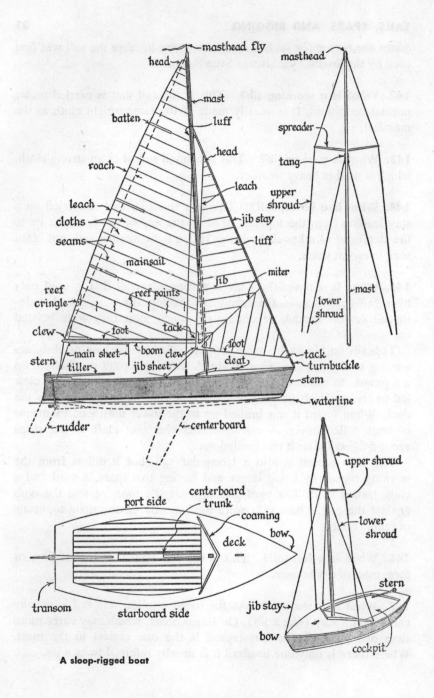

masthead fly

head

masthead

mast

batten

luff

spreader

roach

head

tang

leach

upper
shroud

leach

jib stay

cloths

luff

seams

mast

mainsail

miter

jib

reef
cringle

reef points

lower
shroud

clew

foot

tack

main sheet

boom

clew

foot

tack

stern

tiller

jib sheet

cleat

turnbuckle

stem

waterline

rudder

centerboard

upper shroud

centerboard
trunk

port side

coaming

bow

lower
shroud

deck

stern

transom

starboard side

jib stay

bow

cockpit

A sloop-rigged boat

148. What sail is sometimes called a "cheater"?   The spinnaker staysail, a small sail that is set under the spinnaker when the wind is not too far aft, is sometimes called a cheater. There is nothing illegal about it; it is merely taking advantage of every last place to hoist a sail.

149. Where is a fisherman staysail used?   This quadrilateral sail is hoisted between the masts of a schooner. It has two halyards, one leading to the head of the mainmast, the other to the foremast, near its head. The sail's tack leads to the pin rail or a cleat on the foremast. The sheet leads down and aft. It may be secured to the main boom or to a cleat on deck. A good lead for the sheet would be through a snatch block on the main boom, thence to a cleat on deck.

150. What is a mizzen staysail?   This is a sail rigged from the mizzenmast of a yawl or ketch. It cannot usually be carried when the boat is really close-hauled. These sails are set flying and are sheeted to the mizzen boom. The tack is secured about amidships on the weather (or windward) side of the deck or cabin top.

151. What is a mizzen spinnaker?   A mizzen spinnaker performs the same function and is rigged in the same manner as a mizzen staysail. It is merely cut fuller, more along the lines of an ordinary spinnaker.

152. What is a mule?   This is a staysail that is hoisted on the permanent backstay of a yawl or ketch. It is sheeted to the head of the mizzenmast. It is possible to rig a mule on a sloop that has a permanent backstay, but a stump mast must be fitted at the stern to take the mule's sheet. The latter is an unusual rig, but it has been used.

153. What is a storm trisail?   This is a small, extra heavy sail that is carried in heavy weather in place of the mainsail. Its luff is attached to the mast, but it is loose footed and usually sheets to the outboard end of the mainboom.

154. What is a spinnaker net?   A spinnaker net is usually a series of lines or tapes stretched aloft between the jibstay and the mast to prevent the spinnaker from wrapping around the headstay if it collapses.

There are many different ways in which spinnaker nets may be constructed, but the desired result is the same.

155. What is a miter?   When making triangular sails, such as jibs, staysails, etc., it is customary for the sailmaker to join the upper and lower parts of the sail at a seam that runs across the sail at a broad angle with the stay on which it is mounted. The angle of the miter is determined by the angle made where the foot and leech of the sail join at the clew. The miter bisects this angle and extends from this point to the stay. Its purpose is to help insure the sail's ability to withstand a tendency to stretch out of shape.

With a staysail that is rigged to a boom it is not usual to have a miter in the sail.

156. What is a cringle?   A cringle is a loop or eye worked into the edge of a sail so that it can be secured at that point with a suitable lashing. Cringles on large sails are usually made from rope and may project from the sail's edge. In small sails a hole is punched in the sailcloth and carefully hand stitched all around to reinforce it. All cringles are lined with metal—usually brass—grommets or thimbles.

157. What is a grommet?   As used on yachts a grommet is a two-piece brass liner used to reinforce a hole made by the sailmaker in a piece of fabric such as a sail or awning.

158. Is there another kind of grommet?   Yes. Another type of grommet which can be quite handy for certain purposes is formed by unlaying a piece of three-strand rope and then relaying a single strand around itself to form a ring or circle. It must be relaid until it forms a three-strand rope and the two ends of the strand are tucked under each other plus one or two more strands, as in splicing. The ends are then cut off short.

A strand about three and a half times the diameter of the finished grommet must be used.

159. What is a chafe patch?   Chafe patches are used on sails in places where they may have a tendency to come in contact with and wear against a fixed object such as a spreader or a shroud. They are generally an extra thickness of sailcloth placed where they will be most effective.

160. What is a batten pocket? A batten pocket is one of three or four long, rectangular fabric receptacles sewn at 90 degrees to the leech of a sail for the purpose of holding a batten.

161. What is the function of a batten? Battens support the leech of a sail so that it may include roach or convex curvature.

162. How long should battens be in relation to their batten pockets? A batten should be about one inch shorter than its pocket, or of a length that will slide in and secure easily. It should not be so loose, however, that it damages or rips the sail by working.

163. Is it a good idea to paint or varnish battens? Yes, this will keep the battens from absorbing water which adds weight and makes them difficult to remove because of swelling.

164. Why are sails made of many cloths sewn together? Seams are necessary to control sail shape and stretch. And there are no looms capable of weaving cloth wide enough to make a seamless sail.

165. What is meant when we say, for example, that a sail is made five-ounce sailcloth? This is the United States standard for describing a piece of the material 28½ inches wide by 36 inches long and weighing five ounces.

166. Of what sailcloth weights are sails commonly made? The lightest spinnakers are made from a nylon material weighing 0.5 ounce. Working sails for the largest sailboats afloat today are made from 18- or 20-ounce material. A 12-meter boat's mainsail is normally of 12-ounce material, while she will have Genoas weighing from 3 to 9 ounces, which are used according to wind velocity. The smaller racing classes have mainsails and jibs made of 3- to 6-ounce materials.

167. What type of fabrics are used for sailcloth? Spinnakers are made of a tightly woven nylon that has a smooth, hard surface, achieved by applying heat and pressure in the finishing process. Most other sails are now made from Dacron, a registered trademark of Du-Pont for its polyester fiber from which the material is woven. Very few sails are made today from any of the natural fibers such as cotton, synthetics having proved superior.

168. Why is synthetic sailcloth generally considered superior?   Synthetic sailcloth requires no "breaking in" as had to be done with cotton sails. It will not absorb or hold water and thus may be stored damp without danger from mildew damage if clean and salt-free. Probably most important, synthetic sails will hold their built-in shape for a long time, a vital consideration for the racing man.

169. Can the shape of a sail be improved or changed after it has been built?   Yes. A sail can be "re-cut" by removing stitching along a seam and resewing it in a different position. This is common practice, especially among racing sailors.

170. How long will synthetic sails last?   This is difficult to answer, since it depends on the use and treatment the sail receives. Ordinarily, a synthetic sail should last and be effective for at least five or six seasons of average use. Aboard cruising boats ten years service or longer is not unusual.

171. Does sunlight effect nylon and Dacron?   Under normal use, sunlight will have very little effect on either nylon or Dacron. The latter is said to resist the sunlight better, but exposure to it is not a serious problem.

172. Does heat adversely affect synthetic sails?   Not unless you bake them in an oven. Cigarette burns, however, can cause damage in a limited area.

173. Should the outhaul on Dacron mainsails be eased off when not sailing?   Yes. This gives your sails a chance to rest. They will last longer and hold their shape better on boats where mainsails are furled on the boom; if the outhaul is slacked.

174. What is the proper way to furl a sail? First, of course, the sail has to be lowered all the way and its outhaul is slacked. It is then pushed all to one side of the boom, usually to port. The crew now lines up on the opposite side of the boom and pulls over sufficient cloth along the boom to encompass the entire body of the sail. This takes a bit of judgment, which only comes with practice. Now, working in unison, the main body of the sail is pulled toward the crewmen and tucked and pounded (in the case of large sails) into the fold or trough formed by the cloth originally pulled over. Then, the whole bundle of cloth, which should be tightly rolled by this time, is rolled up on top of the boom, and the stops or gaskets are passed around it to hold it securely. If the sail has slides along its foot it is usual to make the first pass of the stop between the sail and the boom. The second pass (and third, if the stop is a long one) goes around both sail and boom. Finally, after pulling it very tight, a bow is tied in the stop.

If the boom is equipped with shock-cord furling, the stops are eliminated and the cord is simply passed over the sail to the waiting hooks on the boom's opposite side.

175. What are sail stops, or gaskets? Sail stops are fabric straps used to lash a sail to its boom when the sail is furled.

176. How often should sails be inspected? At the end of each season it is a good idea to have a sailmaker go over your sails to check for such things as worn stitching, bent fittings, chafe, tears, and rips. The wise skipper also checks over his sails for some of these items each time they are used.

177. Is it a good idea to wash synthetic sails? Yes, especially when they become dirty or covered with salt. A sail that looks well will usually perform better. A mild detergent mixed with water and a reasonably stiff brush are all that is necessary. It is important that the soap be rinsed off. Stains and spots should not be removed without first consulting your sailmaker. Many cleaning fluids can do permanent damage to the fabric.

It is also a good idea to keep sail bags clean. They can mildew if salt and dirt accumulate.

178. Is it a good idea to fold or roll sails before stowing?   Because of the hard finish of Dacron sailcloth, it will wrinkle easily. Therefore it is common practice with small sails where it is easily accomplished to fold and roll sails carefully to keep wrinkles to a minimum.

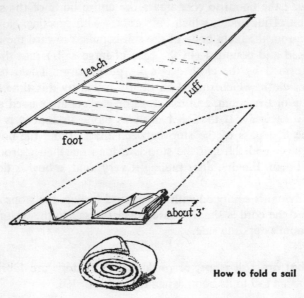

leach

luff

foot

about 3'

How to fold a sail

179. Where and how should sails be stored when not in use? After sails have been inspected, cleaned, and dried, they should be folded neatly and placed in a clean sail bag. Synthetic sails like to breathe, so they should not be packed too tightly. They are best kept in a well-ventilated, vermin-free, dry area.

180. What are spars?   The term "spars" embraces the masts, booms, gaffs, bowsprits, and spinnaker poles of sailboats and the signal masts of powerboats.

181. Of what materials are spars usually made?   For wooden spar spruce is the first choice, fir, second. Extruded aluminum spars are becoming increasingly popular.

182. How are wooden masts made?   On small sailboats wood masts are usually made solid, but hollow masts are common on the larger sizes. These are glued in pieces and may be of round, oval, or box section. No fastenings are used in forming hollow masts, the pieces being held together entirely by glue.

183. How are aluminum masts made? They are extruded. That is, the molten aluminum is forced through a die which gives the mast its finished shape. It comes out as a long tube and is then cut to the length required. Squeezing toothpaste from a tube is extrusion in its simplest form.

184. What are the advantages of aluminum masts? They are stronger than wooden masts of the same dimensions and are lighter than solid wooden masts. If they are anodized, they need no care except an occasional wiping off with a damp cloth.

185. What are the disadvantages of aluminum masts? They cost more than comparable wooden spars. Aluminum being heavier than water, a boat with an aluminum mast may turn bottom-up if it capsizes, whereas with a wooden mast it would lay on its side. The slatting of running rigging against a mast when the wind blows can be annoying. With an aluminum mast it is particularly so, as the clanking set up when wire halyards slap against the spar sounds like a blacksmith shop.

186. Can aluminum spars be filled to reduce noise? Yes. Foam materials have been successfully used to fill the interiors of aluminum masts. This reduces noise considerably and also can prevent the spar from filling with water if the boat capsizes.

187. Has titanium ever been used as a material for masts? Yes. The 1964 America's Cup defender *Constellation* had an experimental mast, the top 36 feet of which were titanium. The main advantage of this material is that it will bend four times as far as aluminum before breaking, but it costs fourteen times as much.

188. What are the parts of a mast? The lower end of a mast is called the foot. The projection that fits into the mast step is the tenon. The top of a mast is called the masthead. Some wooden mastheads are finished off with a wooden fitting called a truck. This usually has holes or a sheave in it for reeving a flag halyard. Aluminum masts for small boats often have a groove which takes the sail's luff rope. This groove is extruded integrally with the spar when it is made and is called, simply, the slot or groove. Wood masts are sometimes made this way too, but this means they must be hollow. Usually wood masts are fitted with a mast track to take the slides on the luff of the sail.

189. What is a mast step? This is a term used to describe the structural member on which the mast stands. It runs fore and aft and usually spans several frames. At its center is a rectangular hole, or mortise, to fit the tenon of the mast. The mast step is usually made of white oak, but in some modern "goldplaters" it is made of a metal—bronze or steel—weldment.

190. What is meant by mast partners? This is the area of the deck through which the mast passes. The space between the deck and the mast is normally filled with blocks of wood or rubber for support and then made watertight with a canvas or rubber boot.

191. What causes masts to fail? Excessive wind pressure on the sails set up tremendous stresses in a mast and its rigging. Sometimes the rigging parts, which usually causes the mast to break off for lack of support. Occasionally a spreader fails, and this too can cause the spar to break.

Perhaps the most common cause of breakage, at least in big boats, is compression. Technically, a mast is a column that must be of sufficient strength to withstand the force applied to it when wind pressure on the sails sets up great tension on the weather shrouds. This causes an equal compressive force on the spar. If this force is great enough, and the spar is not of sufficient diameter, it will buckle, and perhaps fracture, below the shrouds.

192. What precautions should be taken each season before the first sail of a wood-planked boat? A boat should if possible have at least a few days to allow its planking to swell before the mast is stepped. It is not necessary, however, to wait so long as with a new boat.

During the first sail of the season a wood boat should never be driven hard. Shrouds should be set up just enough to keep the mast in place, and windward work should be avoided.

193. How long should one wait after launching before stepping the mast of a new wood boat? It is advisable to wait at least a week to give the new hull a chance to swell. This restriction, of course, does not apply to fiber-glass or metal boats.

194. How should a mast be stored? When out of a boat, a mast should always be placed in a horizontal position so that it is well supported along its entire length. If it is not, it is likely to develop a permanent sag. Wood masts should be stored where direct sunlight cannot reach them. If they must be stored out of doors they should be well covered.

195. How is rigging defined? A boat's rigging is divided into two categories: standing and running rigging.

Standing rigging, which is usually wire rope (often stainless steel), is permanently rigged to support the masts.

Running rigging consists of fiber rope such as manila, nylon, or Dacron. It usually runs through blocks and is used to hoist and control sails.

196. How is standing rigging identified? Wire rigging that supports a mast in a fore-and-aft direction is called a stay—i.e., jibstay, forestay, backstay. Wire rigging supporting a mast athwartships is called a shroud—i.e., lower shroud, upper shroud, topmast shroud, bowsprit shroud.

197. How are stays and shrouds attached to spars and hulls? Their upper ends are attached to metal fittings called tangs, their lower ends to chain plates bolted to the hull.

198. What is a tang? This is a metal fitting bolted to a mast to which shrouds and stays are attached. Tangs are usually made of high tensile strength stainless steel or bronze. Their design and attachment are critical, as the strength and reliability of a yacht's entire rig depends on their not failing. The failure of a tang under stress is very likely to result in the breaking of a mast.

199. What is a chain plate? The upper ends of the shrouds and stays which support a mast are attached to tangs, the lower ends to

chain plates. Chain plates are securely bolted to the hull structure
which is strengthened at the point where they attach. Shroud chain
plates may run down either outside or inside the hull planking. On
modern yachts they usually are inside. Chain plates at bow and stern
are bolted to the outside of the stem and transom. Like tangs, they
are usually made of high tensile strength stainless steel or bronze.

200. What is a turnbuckle? As wire rigging (stays and shrouds)
requires adjustment, it is necessary to provide some means of doing
this. The usual way is by the use of turnbuckles. At the lower end of
each piece of wire rigging supporting a mast, a turnbuckle is introduced between the wire and the chain plate.

Turnbuckles consist of three parts, a body and two screws which fit
the body. One screw has a right-hand thread, the other has a left-
hand thread. By turning the body, the overall length of a turnbuckle
can be varied as required.

The ends of the screws are designed to be attached to the wire at
one end and the chain plate at the other.

To prevent turnbuckles from unscrewing under strain it is usual to
insert cotter pins through holes in the end of each screw after adjustment is completed. As the ends of these pins might tear a sail, it is
usual to wrap protective tape around the turnbuckle to cover the
points of the cotter pins.

Some turnbuckles are made with lock nuts instead of cotter pins.
There are also some patented types which require neither pins nor
nuts.

201. What is a spreader? Spreaders are used on a mast to keep
shrouds at an advantageous angle for maximum support. They are
often made of the same material as the mast—either wood or metal
—and mounted athwartships at right angles to the mast.

202. What is a jumper strut? A jumper strut is a type of spreader
on the fore side of the mast that is used to support the upper part of
the mast. It is generally found on boats that do not have a headstay
going to the top of the mast.

203. What is a triatic stay? This is the stay that runs between the
tops of the masts on a two-masted vessel.

204. What is the difference between a forestay and a headstay?
A headstay is led to the bow of a boat, whereas a forestay is located
further inboard. Both may carry sails. The headstay also often goes
to a point higher on the mast.

If a Genoa jib is in use on the headstay of a boat that also has a
forestay, the latter must be removable quickly and easily to allow
tacking.

205. What are running backstays?   Running backstays are used to
support a mast from aft that also has a forestay on which they maintain tension. There are two running backstays, port and starboard,
and they lead to either quarter of the boat. When under sail only the
windward one is used. At anchor they are both set up to give a shipshape appearance and afford added support to the mast.

**206. Why do many modern ocean racers have no running back-
stays?**   It has been found that, with modern materials, running backstays are often no longer necessary. Forestays and running backstays
usually go together and attach to the same general area of a mast. If a
rig lacks one, it usually lacks the other.

On yachts with permanent backstays and headstays which reach
only about seven-eighths of the mast's height from the deck, running
backstays can be eliminated by substituting a jumper strut at the
point where the headstay attaches to the mast, and rigging twin
jumper stays over this strut, which is usually V-shaped to take the
stays over its two forward-extending legs. By this means running
backstays, which are a nuisance to handle, can be eliminated.

207. What is bar rigging?   This is a solid stainless steel type of
standing rigging that is more rigid than the customary stranded wire
rigging. And it is vastly more expensive.

208. Why is proper tuning of the rigging important?   Unless standing rigging is properly tuned, a boat will not sail her best. Considerable variation can be achieved in the set of sails according to how the
rigging is tuned.

209. Where does one start in tuning?   Begin by setting up the upper
shrouds and then adjust the lowers. By sighting up the mast you can
tell the effect of each adjustment.

210. What is the first and most important requirement of a properly tuned mast?   Any well-tuned mast is completely straight athwartships when sailing close-hauled. This is achieved by adjusting the tension on the shrouds.

211. After preliminary tuning, what should you do?   Go for a sail. Sight up the mast to be sure it is straight on both tacks. If it is not, luff up and make adjustments. It is not good practice to adjust turnbuckles that are under heavy load, as this is apt to strip the threads.

212. What is the primary objective of all tuning?   To keep the mast straight and the headstay as taut as possible, so that jibs will have a straight leading edge for effective windward sailing.

213. What precautions must be taken in tuning?   One must be careful not to get the rigging overly tight. Abnormal tension is apt to cause gear failures. Standing rigging should not be so taut as to sound like the strings of a violin.

214. Which shrouds carry the greatest load?   The upper shrouds. Consequently they must be adjusted more taut than the lower shrouds.

215. How should a permanent backstay be adjusted?   A permanent backstay should be set up so that the mast is absolutely straight, with no forward bend.

216. How can a mainsail be flattened by adjusting the backstay?   When the permanent backstay is tightened on a masthead rig, the mast bows slightly, its head moves aft and its midsection forward. This flattens the sail and reduces its draft or curvature.

217. Will wire standing rigging stretch?   Yes. Particularly when it is new, wire rope rigging will stretch to a surprising extent. This fact should be kept in mind, for tuning is a season-long chore.

218. What is baggy wrinkle?   This is a term that refers to chafing gear placed on standing rigging where sails rub against it.

219. Why are shroud rollers used?   Such rollers are designed to speed the passage by the shrouds of sheets and large headsails when tacking, and to reduce friction between these components.

220. Of what materials are shroud rollers made?   In most cases, any plastic hose will do very nicely. Also often used are bamboo poles. Fancier, but not necessarily more durable, rollers may be made of aluminum tubes. Two-piece rollers, split longitudinally, having a central hole for the shroud, are made of ash or other durable wood, the halves being bound together, as required, with adhesive tape or marline.

221. What should be done to the standing rigging before the mast is removed at the end of a season?   It is a good idea to mark the buckles with tape to indicate their position when the mast was properly tuned. These marks will serve as excellent reference points to begin tuning the following season. And, of course, every item should be tagged for easy identification next season.

222. How is running rigging classified?   It is divided into groups by function—halyards, sheets, downhauls, topping lifts, outhauls, lazyjacks, brails, and runners, for example.

223. What is a halyard?   This is the name given to a rope used to hoist a sail or a flag. The rope that hoists a jib is called a jib halyard; that for a mainsail, the main halyard, etc. On small boats it will be a single rope part, but as sail area increases, wire is usually used and the final strain on the halyard is taken by a winch on the mast. Some wire halyards are rigged on reels, and the sail is hoisted by turning a crank.

Where a wire halyard is manhandled it has a fiber rope (Dacron or manila) tail of larger diameter spliced to its hauling end. This enables the crew to haul on the tail by hand until the wire is reached. At this point the wire is wrapped several times around the winch, and the last few feet are reeled in mechanically.

224. What is a sheet?   This is a rope used to control the angle or trim of a sail in relation to the prevailing wind. It may be single as in a dinghy, or it may be a tackle having blocks and several "parts," the number depending on the area of the sail to be trimmed.

225. What is a downhaul? Some sails, particularly headsails such as jibs and forestaysails, and mainsails are rigged with a rope or wire which performs the reverse of a halyard. This is called a downhaul.

226. What is a topping lift? This is the name given a rope used to support the outer end of a boom. It is adjustable so the boom can be raised or lowered as required. A topping lift can be rigged in two ways: It can be secured to the boom end and led to a block near the masthead, thence to a cleat on the mast near the deck, somewhat like a halyard. Or it can be secured near the masthead, led through a block on the boom end and thence to a cleat on the boom. On larger boats there will be a tackle introduced in the rig.

227. What is an outhaul? A sail whose foot is fitted with a boom has to be hauled out along the boom when the sail is hoisted. Otherwise it would not set properly. The line used to haul the foot of the sail taut is called an outhaul. Rigged from the sail's clew to the end of the boom, it may be a single part on a small boat, or on a big yacht it may be a tackle of several parts.

The outhaul should be slacked off when the sail is lowered.

228. What is a lazyjack? Cruising sailboats are sometimes rigged with rope slings which are attached to the upper part of the mast on each side. These lines lead down and aft to each side of the boom and serve to catch and hold the sail as it is lowered.

Lazyjacks are rigged in various ways, depending on the size of the sail. They are usually adjustable to prevent their cutting across the lee side of a sail full of wind.

229. What is a brail? Certain sails are rigged so they do not lower. They are gathered to the mast and gaff by means of lines which gather them into a compact bundle. These lines are called brails, and a sail so gathered is said to be brailed-up.

This rig is practically obsolete on yachts, but is still used in England and Holland on some work boats.

230. What is a lead?   There are two kinds of lead (rhymes with seed)—fair and foul. When a rope leads clear and without interference it is called a fair-lead. If there is interference it is a foul-lead.

231. What is the general rule on the position of a jib sheet lead? A jib should be trimmed on a line about ten to twelve degrees off the boat's centerline, measured from the jib-tack fitting. On a slow or beamy boat, the angle may be greater, and on a fast narrow one it may be somewhat less.

232. How can you tell where to place a Genoa sheet lead fore and aft?   The genoa's miter is a good guide. Normally the sheet should be an extension of the miter at the same angle leading to the block. In lighter air the lead may be slightly aft of this line, and in heavy air it may be forward of it.

233. What will happen if the Genoa lead is too far aft?   The head of the sail will fall off and flap along the leech. If the lead is too far forward, the leech will appear tight and probably cause excessive backwinding of the mainsail.

234. What are the advantages of synthetic rope over the natural fiber ropes?   Synthetic rope can be made stronger for the same weight. It has a tendency to stretch less (particularly Dacron) and returns to its original dimension more readily. Synthetic rope is also nonabsorbent and thus can be stowed wet without mildewing.

Nylon rope, because of its great elasticity, makes poor running rigging but is excellent for dock lines, for mooring or anchoring, and for towing.

235. Are sheets ever made of both wire and rope?   Yes. On larger boats particularly, rope is often used for the tail or handling part of the sheet, while enough wire is used so that there will be sufficient turns around the winch when the sail is sheeted in tight.

236. Is there a rope made that includes both nylon and Dacron? Yes. The Sampson Cordage Company produces a yacht rope that has a Dacron core covered with braided nylon. This rope can be spliced and is easy on the hands because it is soft and flexible. It makes excellent running rigging.

237. Does tying a knot in a rope reduce its strength?   If a tight knot is tied in a rope it can reduce the rope's strength up to 50 percent. That is why it is always preferable to splice if great strain is likely.

238. What is probably the greatest threat to running rigging? Chafe. It should be guarded against continually and entirely prevented if at all possible.

V. SEAMANSHIP

Introduction. The dictionary defines seamanship as the skill of a good seaman, or skill in navigating a vessel. Such a brief definition hardly scratches the surface of the subject. Seamanship is an all-embracing term and is by far the most important attribute for one who goes on the water—even though only in a sailing dinghy. It is a mixture of experience and a certain natural awareness. A good seaman unconsciously takes note of weather and sea conditions, the state of the tide or current, the force and direction of the wind, the motion of the boat. He is capable of bringing her to anchor under all conditions, and he knows the rules of the road.

He knows sailor's knots and hitches and can splice a rope and repair a sail. He is a good helmsman and can hold a true course, either by compass or by the stars. He will be a good "shipkeeper"; that is, he will always keep his boat neat and clean and shipshape. He is all these things and a lot more. But above all he must love boats and the sea.

239. What are the International Rules of the Road at Sea?   This is a set of rules established to prevent collisions between vessels, both sail and power. The rules were drawn up originally in the days of square-riggers.

240. When two sailboats on opposite tacks are approaching each other on courses that might lead to a collision, which one has the right of way?   The boat on the starboard tack always has the right of way over one on the port tack. The latter must keep clear.

241. When two sailboats are converging on the same tack, and danger of collision exists, which boat must keep clear?   The boat to windward must keep clear because the leeward boat has the right of way.

242. When has a sailboat the right of way over a powerboat? At all times except when the sailboat is the overtaking vessel; then the powerboat has the right of way.

49

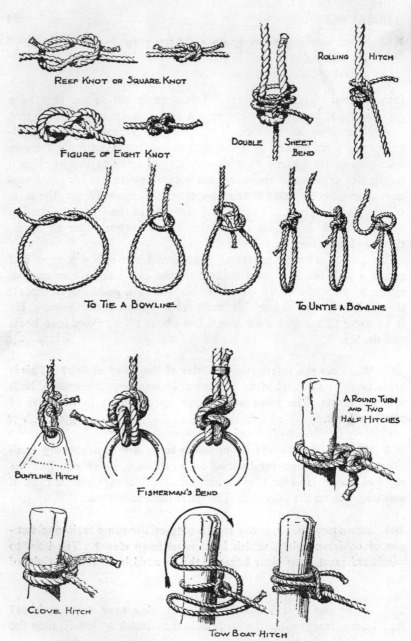

REEF KNOT OR SQUARE KNOT

FIGURE OF EIGHT KNOT

ROLLING HITCH

DOUBLE SHEET BEND

TO TIE A BOWLINE

TO UNTIE A BOWLINE

A ROUND TURN AND TWO HALF HITCHES

BUNTLINE HITCH

FISHERMAN'S BEND

CLOVE HITCH

TOW BOAT HITCH

KNOTS AND HITCHES

243. When does a powerboat have the right of way over a sailboat?
When a sailboat is overtaking a powerboat it must keep clear, because the overtaken vessel has the right of way.

244. If two vessels under power are converging, which has the right of way? The vessel on the other's starboard side has the right of way.

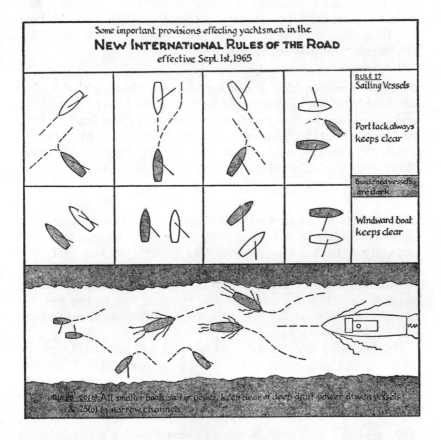

Some important provisions effecting yachtsmen in the
NEW INTERNATIONAL RULES OF THE ROAD
effective Sept. 1st, 1965

RULE 17
Sailing Vessels

Port tack always
keeps clear

Burdened vessels
are dark

Windward boat
keeps clear

RULE 20(b) All smaller boats, sail or power, keep clear of deep draft power driven vessels
& 25(b) in narrow channels

245. How do the International Rules of the Road at sea differ from the racing rules of the North American Yacht Racing Union (NAYRU)? The international rules are intended to prevent collisions, while the NAYRU rules establish the terms under which races are sailed. The latter are so complicated that they occupy a whole book.

246. What is the proper way to approach a mooring? A boat should always be headed directly into the wind when approaching a mooring. This applies to both sail and powerboats. Obviously, a boat should lose way (come to a stop) as the mooring buoy is reached. This is easy to do under power; simply reverse the engine. In a sailboat, however, the helmsman must estimate closely how far his boat will fetch under existing conditions of wind and sea. This knowledge can be gained only by experience.

247. When approaching a mooring in a powerboat, with the wind aft, how is the boat maneuvered to pick up the buoy? Slow down and proceed several boat lengths beyond the buoy, then head the boat up into the wind. Approach the buoy slowly directly upwind, have a boathook handy and someone forward to pick up the buoy. As soon as the mooring line is aboard and secured, reverse the engine for just long enough to get sternway.

248. What is the proper way to pick up a mooring in a sailboat when approaching before the wind? To accomplish this maneuver it is necessary to have a very accurate idea how far the boat will fetch under existing wind and sea conditions. Sail by the buoy, leaving it several boat lengths away from the side opposite to that on which the boom is carried. When the helmsman estimates that he has gone far enough, he puts down his helm slowly, thus swinging the boat's head into the wind in a wide arc.

As she comes head to the wind her sails will luff. Wind pressure then retards her speed instead of driving the boat ahead. If the maneuver is properly performed, the boat's bow will come to rest just over the buoy so it can be picked up easily.

249. When cruising how do you go about choosing an anchorage? In examining your chart and analyzing the weather, pick an anchorage with good holding ground that will afford protection from the anticipated wind direction. Never anchor in channels, and try to avoid areas with strong currents.

250. What is the proper way to anchor a powerboat?   Just as when approaching a mooring, a boat should be brought head to wind before her anchor is let go. And she should be allowed to lose all way (headway) before anchoring. Reversing her engine will accomplish this quickly. As the boat begins to go astern, drop the anchor. This will cause it to dig in or set as the anchor rode is snubbed.

251. How much scope is it advisable to allow?   The amount of scope to be allowed when anchoring varies with conditions. Where there is good holding (mud and clay) less scope will be required than on a poor bottom such as sand or kelp. The ideal scope is about seven times the depth of water at high tide.

252. How can depth of water be determined?   With a sounding lead, a sounding pole or with a sonic depth finder.

253. What precautions are necessary when anchoring in a tidal current?   In anchoring where a strong current might have more effect than the wind (as in a tidal river), care should be taken not to anchor too close to land that could become a lee shore when the current reverses direction.

254. How is the time and range of the tide determined?   In familiar waters it is easy to estimate the time and height of the tide, but when cruising in strange waters it is advisable to consult the government tide tables for reliable information.

255. How does time afford anchoring procedure?   If anchoring only for a short time—say, for lunch or a swim—less scope and a lighter anchor (lunch hook) can be used—that is, assuming the weather is good, that there will be someone on deck to be sure the anchor is not dragging and the bottom is good holding ground.

Obviously, if anchoring for the night or longer, procedure will be different. A heavier anchor should be used than for temporary anchoring, adequate scope should be paid out, and care should be taken to be sure the anchor is not dragging.

256. How can one tell if the anchor is dragging?   There are several ways. One is by taking a range on two fixed objects on shore. Another is by observing nearby fixed objects such as other boats or buoys. Still another way to tell if the anchor is holding is to drop over the side a heavy weight (such as a sounding lead) attached to a piece of light line. Let the weight lie on the bottom and keep the line up-and-down. This will show if the boat is drifting over the bottom. On a dark night, in thick fog, or when out of sight of land this is the best way to detect dragging.

257. How is the nature of the bottom in a strange anchorage determined? Where the water is clear enough, the bottom can usually be seen. In certain areas the type of bottom is a foregone conclusion, but where this information is in doubt, reference should be made to the detail (large-scale) chart of the area. The nature of the bottom is usually shown on such charts.

A sample of the bottom (except rock) can usually be taken by sounding with a lead armed with tallow or cup grease. But perhaps the best way to determine if the anchor is in good holding ground is to put a good strain on it by reversing the engine for a few minutes. If it doesn't drag, it is safe to assume the bottom is good.

258. How can a sailboat with no motor put a strain on an anchor to be sure it is holding? Pushing the mainsail out as far as possible, first on one side, then on the other, will cause a boat to make sternway. This will take up any slack in the anchor rode and put a strain on the anchor. The amount of strain will, of course, depend on the force of the wind.

259. How many anchors should a boat carry? The answer to this depends on the type of boat and her intended use. A small boat, either sail or power, which is used for day sailing will usually carry only one anchor of sufficient weight to hold her in a squall.

A cruising boat, however, which may have to anchor nightly under widely varying conditions, may carry three or more anchors. First, and most important, will be her heavy storm anchor. It should be of a weight and type to hold under the worst conditions to be expected. Actually, such an anchor may be used only occasionally.

Then there is the intermediate or cruising anchor. This is the one that will be most frequently used. It should be light enough to be easily handled, yet have sufficient holding power to serve under normal conditions.

And finally there should be a light anchor which can serve as a "lunch hook" for temporary anchoring or may be useful, under certain conditions, as a stern anchor or as a kedge to help get the boat off a shoal if it should go aground. This one should be of a weight and type that can be carried out in a dinghy, if necessary for kedging.

260. Is there a rule for determining suitable anchor weights for various types of boats?   There is no hard-and-fast rule because conditions vary so greatly from one area to another and the holding power of different anchors also varies considerably. In addition, boats of different types behave differently as they lie to an anchor. For example, a sailboat may lie head-to-wind while a powerboat, in the same conditions, may tend to yaw widely from side-to-side. This puts an extra strain on the anchor.

However, there are certain rule-of-thumb standards that can serve as a rough guide to suitable weights and types of anchors for a given boat and for the kind of bottom to be encountered.

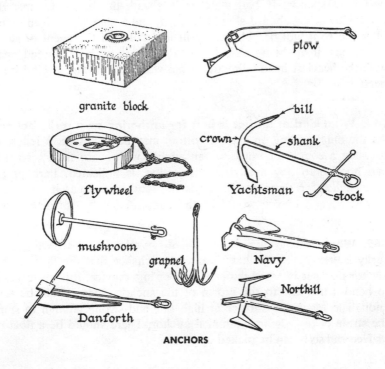

ANCHORS

261. What is the recommended weight of mushroom anchors for sailboats? For heavy cruising types recommended weights vary from seven pounds per foot overall of the boat for small boats to ten pounds per foot for big ones. For lighter racing types of boats figure about 75 percent of the foregoing weights. These figures apply only where boats are moored in well-sheltered harbors with good holding ground.

262. What is the rule for weights of mushroom anchors for power-boats? For power cruisers the recommended weight of a mushroom (mooring) anchor is ten pounds per foot overall of the boat. For small powerboats without cabins, about half the above should be satisfactory in well-sheltered harbors with good holding ground.

263. How does the weather affect anchoring? When anchoring, it is wise to consider the weather conditions to be expected during the period at anchor. If bad weather is ahead, the heaviest, most dependable anchor aboard should be used, and it should be given plenty of scope so it will be able to dig in and hold. In the event of storm conditions, it might be wise to put down two anchors, spread apart with the heaviest in the direction from which the strongest wind is expected.

264. What kind of anchor is best for anchoring on a rocky bottom? As the only holding on such a bottom may be a crevice, a ledge, or between a couple of boulders, an anchor with sharp flukes, so they can hook onto any available obstruction, is indicated. Perhaps the best anchor for these conditions is the sand anchor, as it has sharp points. Second choice would be the conventional "yachtsman" type.

265. What precautions should be observed when anchoring on a rocky bottom? Since there is always a chance that the fluke of the anchor may get jammed under a rock or in a crevice, it is always wise to bend a trip line to the crown of the anchor. This should be long enough to reach the surface at high tide and strong enough to stand the strain of dislodging a jammed anchor. There should be a float on its free end so it can be picked up.

266. How can the normal holding power of an anchor be increased?
By hanging a weight on the rode or cable.

267. How much weight is recommended? It has been found by experiment that a weight equal to about one pound per foot overall of a boat's length is very effective in preventing an anchor from dragging. Any kind of weight will do (a small anchor, for example). In extremely heavy weather more weight would be advisable.

268. How is a weight rigged on an anchor cable? There is a fitting called a Dorham Roderider which makes it easy to hang a weight on an anchor rode. It is designed to prevent abrasion of the rope and can be used on chain as well. Weight is hung from the Roderider and lowered down the cable by means of a check line to a position midway between the boat and its anchor. The use of such a device relieves the tug on an anchor due to storm conditions.

269. What is an anchor cable? A cable may be rope, a chain, or a combination of each. In the case of a permanent mooring, it may also be stainless steel wire rope.

270. What is a rode? A length of rope used for anchoring is called a rode.

271. What rope is considered superior for an anchor rode? Nylon.

272. What can be done to extend the life of an anchor rode? Since only one short section of the line ever gets much use, it is a good idea to "end-for-end" the line each season to equalize exposure and wear.

273. When habitually anchoring on a rocky bottom or among coral heads, what type anchor cable is recommended? Chain.

274. When anchoring temporarily on a rocky bottom or among coral heads, what precaution is recommended to protect an anchor cable from abrasion? The use of chain between the anchor and the anchor rode will prevent abrasion of the latter. Use enough chain so the rode does not touch bottom. Better still, under such conditions use all chain.

275. When anchoring with chain cable, what precautions should be observed?   As chain will run out of its own weight, it is advisable to let out enough at first only to allow the anchor to take hold. As the yacht backs down to set anchor, pay out more chain slowly until the desired scope is reached. Take care not to let the chain pile up on top of the anchor, as it may foul the flukes and cause it to drag.

276. How can an anchor chain be marked to show how much scope has been paid out?   There are various ways of marking chain, but if the first mark is applied at 5 fathoms (30 feet) and subsequent marks at intervals of about the same distance, it becomes easy to tell how much scope is out.

Some paint the links: one link, 5 fathoms; two links, 10 fathoms, etc. Or a piece of marline can be tied around a link as required. Knots can be tied in the marline to indicate scope: one knot, 5 fathoms, etc. Some go in for different colored paint, such as white for 5 fathoms, green for 10 fathoms, red for 15 fathoms, etc.

277. How can an anchor rode be marked to show how much scope has been paid out?   The same system as described for marking chain can be used. The important points to remember are that the system used should be simple so anyone can tell its meaning, and the marks should be easy to see (or feel) in the dark.

278. What paints can be used to mark anchor rodes and chains?   There is a paint available in hobby shops in small bottles called Testor enamel. It comes in a great many colors and will serve well to mark anchor cables if various colors are wanted.

For a single color, white is recommended, as it can be seen best in the dark. One of the rubber base house paints, which are very tough, might be worth trying.

279. What is a sea anchor?   This is a device for retarding the drift of a boat under stress of heavy weather. It is usually conical in shape and is made of very heavy canvas. The large end is spread open by a strong iron ring to which a hawser is secured. A trip line is secured to the apex of the cone so the sea anchor can be retrieved.

280. How is a sea anchor used? It is usually rigged from the bow of a vessel, like an ordinary anchor, to keep her head to the wind. Under certain conditions it may be rigged from the stern, as some vessels will not lie-to head to wind.

281. What is the effect of using oil in storms? Properly used, oil has a calming effect, particularly on cresting seas which might poop a vessel.

282. What does poop mean? This is a sea term to describe the action of a big following sea which floods the cockpit and deck of a vessel from astern. This can be very dangerous in storm conditions.

283. How much oil is required to produce the desired effect? Very little. A big ship requires only from one to eight quarts per hour. A yacht would need only a very small amount.

284. How is oil used most effectively? There are several ways of spreading oil on stormy seas. A canvas bag (the more loosely woven the better) stuffed with cotton waste and filled with oil can be towed some distance from the vessel. The best distance can be determined only by trial.

Or a gallon can of oil with a few small holes punched in it can be towed. There have been cases reported where oil was fed out through the ship's toilet.

Oil can even be poured overside in an emergency.

285. What kind of oil is most effective? Either vegetable or animal oils—such as turpentine, olive, linseed, cottonseed (vegetable), or fish oil (animal)—are best. Mineral oils—diesel fuel, kerosene, lubricating oils—tend to congeal, but they are better than nothing in an emergency.

286. What is the effect of towing long ropes astern in heavy seas? Like oil, this has the effect of calming the waves and preventing seas from breaking on deck.

287. What does it mean to be hove to?   When in heavy weather a vessel reduces sail almost entirely, and backs and fills with the rudder hard over, she is said to be "hove to."

288. What is the best way to ride out a storm?   The most important things to remember are to reduce speed by whatever means are necessary and to prevent waves from breaking on deck. By experimentation with a particular boat in various conditions, you will find out whether she rides best running before the storm, with seas abeam, or headed directly into the seas.

289. What is the most important rule to remember if bad weather, such as a sudden squall, seems to be approaching?   Be prepared. You don't necessarily have to drop sail and wait for the wind and rain to come, but you should always be ready for anything. Be organized and think ahead to what action will be required if bad weather suddenly should hit.

290. What do barometers indicate?   Barometers record atmospheric pressure which changes as frontal systems pass. The change in the reading is the only important factor. A rise or a fall in pressure indicates a change from existing conditions.

291. If the barometer falls rapidly what is indicated?   You should expect a storm. If the barometer falls rapidly a great distance you may be involved with a severe storm of hurricane intensity.

292. What is the meaning of the expression "Red sky at night, sailors' delight; red in the morning, sailors take warning"?   For many years sailors have believed that if there is a red sunset, the next day will bring clear skies and fair winds. If, on the other hand, the sun rises red, the belief has been that the day will bring foul weather. Try applying this to your observations. You'll be amazed at the number of times it holds true.

293. What is the safest way to handle a small boat under power in head seas?   Head the boat into the waves at a slight angle to avoid pounding. Enough power should be used so that the action of the waves does not toss the bow around. Maintain steerageway at all times, if possible.

294. Is it possible to enter inlets in a heavy following sea? Yes, but it is dangerous and extreme care must be taken that the boat does not get broadside to the waves. There should be sufficient speed for control, but the bow should not bury in the wave ahead as the vessel runs down a wave.

295. What is a safety belt or harness? As the name implies, this is worn by an individual to keep himself on board a vessel at sea. They should always be worn at night and any time conditions are rough. Safety belts normally have a snap hook at the end of a lanyard for clipping on to such convenient gear as lifelines.

296. What advice would you give someone who said they wanted to sail around the world? Be sure they know what they are getting into. Inexperienced persons sometimes get to sea and find they really don't like it at all. If a person has never been to sea in a small boat for an extended period, it is best to have him try at least a short cruise before setting off on a longer voyage.

297. When you are to be a cruising guest for the first time, what should you remember? Never take suitcases aboard boats; there is not room for storing them. Bring bags that can be folded into a small space.

298. What is meant by lee bowing the current? Tidal current under the lee bow of a boat will move it to windward. When racing, considerable distance can be gained by knowledge of how a current flows and by putting it to good use. For example, you can tack before reaching the lay-line to a mark and still fetch it with lift received from the current.

299. What should be remembered in backing a single screw vessel? A single propeller will tend to swing the stern of a boat to port.

300. How is ship's bell time told?

Bells	Time		
1	4:30	8:30	12:30
2	5:00	9:00	1:00
3	5:30	9:30	1:30
4	6:00	10:00	2:00
5	6:30	10:30	2:30
6	7:00	11:00	3:00
7	7:30	11:30	3:30
8	8:00	12:00	4:00

Bells (except one bell) should be struck in groups of two: thus, 00-00-00-0 (7 bells)

VI. DESIGN AND CONSTRUCTION

Introduction. To the dedicated yachtsman the design and construction of boats, be they sail or power, constitute one of the most fascinating aspects of the sport. With the exception of a few gifted amateurs, however, the designing of yachts is left largely in the hands of professional naval architects or yacht designers, whose hulls often have such distinctive characteristics that they can be easily recognized by the initiated. In the yachting fraternity the names of well-known yacht designers are household words. And how sailing yacht hull forms have changed over the years. Such changes having been encouraged by the provisions of certain measurement rules—notably the rules of the Cruising Club of America—which penalize features of design that either are regarded as undesirable or give the yacht possessing them an advantage over her adversaries. The result of such limitations has been the development of a large fleet of racing and cruising boats with characteristics of seaworthiness and speed that would have been unusual a generation ago. To be sure, there have been fast sailing yachts for the better part of a century. And there were seaworthy yachts, but the combination of speed and seaworthiness was seldom to be found in the same vessel.

Powerboat design has undergone as big a transformation as that of sailing yachts. In the early years of this century, when the gasoline engine was being introduced for marine use, a 40-foot cruiser might have had a three-cylinder, 14 horsepower engine which would deliver a snappy 8 knots—that is, if it ran. Today a 37-footer ran from Miami, Florida, to New York, stopping only for fuel, in a matter of 46 hours, 23 minutes and at sea the whole way. And smaller offshore racing boats dash across the Gulf Stream from Miami to Nassau—a distance of 160 miles—in less than four hours.

But perhaps the development of reliable outboard motors has had the greatest effect on powerboat design, both open boats and small cruisers. Little puddle jumpers leap over the waves at fantastic speeds with their hulls airborne, only their propellers in the water, while more sedate 20-foot cruisers take whole families for extended vacations.

In the same period there has been a revolution in building methods

63

and materials. It is not so many years since wood was the only boat-building material used to any extent in the United States. Now, although wood is still the choice of many knowledgeable yachtsmen for custom-built boats, fiber glass, steel, and aluminum—particularly fiber glass—are taking over an increasing share of the boatbuilding market. And this has had a profound effect on the design of boats, as the material permits the designer more latitude in the choice of hull form. With smaller outboard hulls the result has not always been a happy one, as some pretty weird boats of questionable seaworthiness have been produced and sold to novice buyers in recent years. Before buying a boat in this category it is wise to make sure that she has been designed by a competent man.

The development of new corrosion-resistant aluminum alloys has lead to the building of more large custom offshore racing yachts in the 1960's, and it seems as though this trend will continue and perhaps spread into the smaller sizes. The use of this material for cabin houses and other deck erections on power yachts is also on the increase.

301. Of what does a set of naval architect's plans consist?   A complete set of architect's plans for a yacht includes lines, construction drawings, sail, rigging and spar plans (if a sail boat), a list of scantlings, a table of offsets, plus any additional drawings, such as piping and wiring layouts, that may be required.

302. When we speak of a boat's lines, what is meant?   To the layman, the term simply means her appearance. If the boat pleases him, he says she has nice lines. But to the yacht designer the term "lines" means the drawing on paper showing the form of a boat's hull, which he calls a set of lines.

303. How does a yacht designer draw a set of lines?   To represent a three-dimensional object with an irregular shape, like a boat's hull, on a flat surface, requires at least three views: top view, side view, and end view. These views are called respectively the half-breadth plan, the profile, and the body plan. Every designer has his own methods, but usually the profile will be the first to be drawn. This determines the appearance of the yacht.

After the profile, the designer may draw the midship section. Next might come the half-breadth plan (as a boat's hull is the same on both sides, it is necessary to represent only one side on paper). This plan reveals the shape of the hull as seen from above or below.

Finally, he may draw the body plan, of which the midship section represents the form of the hull amidships as viewed from either end.

304. What are waterlines?   These are theoretical sections of a hull (drawn parallel to the load waterline). Each one reveals the shape of the hull at a given level as seen from below. The load (or designed) waterline is the plane at which the boat is supposed to float. Other waterlines are designated as above or below the load waterline (LWL). Usually these are drawn at regular intervals and are designated as 1 above, 2 above, etc., or 1 below, 2 below, etc.

Waterlines appear as long easy curves on the half-breadth plan and as straight, parallel, horizontal lines on the profile and body plan drawings.

305. What is meant by the load waterline (LWL)?   This is the line along a vessel's hull where air and water meet when the vessel is on an even keel in smooth water. Technically, it is a datum line used by designers to locate positions on a boat's plans as being so far above or below the load waterline. It is also referred to as the designed waterline, but the layman usually calls it simply the waterline.

306. What is the purpose of diagonals?   These lines, which radiate from the center line in the body plan, most nearly approach the curves assumed by the boat's planking. Thus they serve to aid the architect in determining the fairness of his sections and waterlines. Diagonals appear as long curved lines in the half-breadth plan. Usually they are drawn below the center line, while the waterlines are drawn above it.

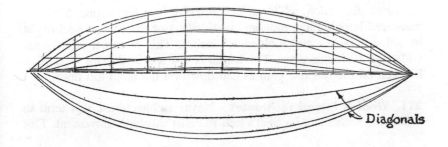

Diagonals

307. What are the buttock lines?   In a sense they are akin to water-lines, except that they are drawn in a vertical plane, parallel to the center line of the yacht. They appear as curved lines in the profile drawing, as straight vertical lines in the body plan, and as evenly spaced lines paralleling the center line on the half-breadth plan. They aid the yacht designer in determining if his other lines are fair.

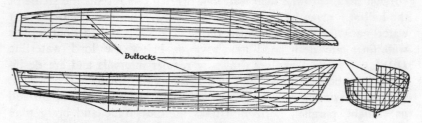

308. What is the purpose of the construction drawings?   The answer to this is fairly obvious. These drawings are made to help the builder to follow accurately the designer's intentions in building a yacht. The more complete the information on the construction plans, the more likely is the owner to get what he wants in the finished yacht. If the designer leaves too much to the builder, the owner may be surprised at the results.

309. What is meant by scantlings?   This is simply the term used by designers and builders to describe the dimensions of a hull's wooden components. A list of scantlings includes the size and spacing of frames, the thickness and depth of other structural members such as the keel, stem, deadwood, floors, clamps, stringers, deck beams, planking, decking, and other components.

310. How are scantlings expressed?   The dimensions of sections of timber are defined as "sided" and "molded." Sided usually refers to the small dimension, while molded refers to the larger one. Siding is measured horizontally; molding, vertically. For example, a keel might be sided 8 inches and molded 10 inches. This means it is 8 inches wide and 10 inches deep. The length is not specified. This dimension is taken off the full size plan as laid down on the mold loft floor.

311. What is lateral resistance?   Naval architects use this term to define the tendency of a boat's hull to resist sideways movement. This tendency can be increased by including in her design one of the following features: a keel, a centerboard, bilgeboards, or lee boards.

312. What is meant by the center of lateral resistance? This is the location in a fore-and-aft direction on a sailboat's hull, representing on the profile drawing the center of gravity of a plane outlined by the profile of the boat from the waterline down, omitting the rudder. This location is designated as the CLR on a yacht's plans.

313. How does one find the center of lateral resistance? This center can be found by calculation, but the simplest way is to cut from a piece of cardboard the profile of the hull below the waterline, omitting the rudder. Lay this across a sharp edge and where it balances is the CLR.

If a boat's plans are not available, her CLR can be approximated by pushing her sideways in the water. Where applied pressure moves her evenly would be near her CLR.

314. What is the significance of the center of lateral resistance in a sailboat? If a boat is to sail well, it must balance; that is, the relationship of its sails to the underwater portion of the hull must be such that there is little or no weather helm, and certainly no lee helm. To accomplish this result, the designer must locate the center of effort (CE) of the sail plan in correct relation to the center of lateral resistance (CLR) of the hull. This is a highly technical problem and one requiring a good deal of experience.

315. What is meant by a boat's center of gravity (CG)? This is a theoretical point at which a boat and all it contains would balance if it were placed on a pivot.

When in water a boat will float so that the center of gravity and the center of buoyancy coincide both fore and aft and athwartships.

The center of gravity is a fixed point, but the center of buoyancy moves as the boat heels or pitches. It may be regarded for the purpose of calculation as the point at which the boat's total weight is concentrated.

316. What is meant by center of buoyancy (CB)? This is a theoretical point at which, for purposes of calculation, yacht designers consider the total buoyancy of a boat to be concentrated. It moves as the boat changes its position owing to heeling or pitching. It is apparent that as a boat's center of gravity (CG) is fixed while its center of buoyancy (CB) is not, the downward thrust at the CG and the upward thrust at the CB (both forces being the same) cause what is called a "righting arm." This tends to keep the boat on an even keel and is referred to as stability.

317. What is stability? The characteristics of a boat's hull that cause it to resist heeling over are summed up in the word stability. Certain forces are always at work to cause a boat to capsize—the weight of spars and all above-water components, plus wind pressure, for example. Opposed to these negative forces are positive forces— the boat's beam (width) plus her ballast, if any. The less permanent ballast she carries, the greater must be her beam. A narrow boat needs a heavy keel. That is why centerboard boats are beamier (wider) than keelboats.

318. What is meant by displacement? This is the total weight of a boat, including everything on board. When in the water, a boat will displace exactly the same weight of water as her own weight.

If you put a model boat into a tub of water that is full to the brim, the water that runs over will be found to weigh exactly the same as the model. This will be true, of course, of any floating object.

319. What is a sail plan? This is a drawing showing the shape of all the sails of a yacht and giving the dimensions of each. It also specifies the weight and kind of sailcloth to be used. The sail plan is often combined with the rigging plan. Weights and areas of sails and rigging sizes are given in a table on the drawing. The yacht's spars are indicated on the sail plan, but their details are given on a separate drawing called the spar plan.

320. What is meant by the term "fore triangle"? This is the area on a sailing yacht bounded by the foremost mast, the deck, and the outermost jibstay.

321. What is the rigging plan? As the name implies this plan shows the leads and specifies the sizes of both standing and running rigging.

It should also specify the sizes and types of blocks, turnbuckles, and other rigging details. This plan is often combined with the sail plan.

322. What is a spar plan? The proper design of a yacht's spars requires great care and knowledge. A mast, in particular, is a critical component.

An unstayed mast, like that of a catboat, only has to be strong enough to stand the bending stress set up by wind pressure on the sail. There are tables giving the tensile strength of woods from which a designer can determine the proper size to make a spar withstand the maximum stress to which it will be subjected.

But the design of a stayed mast is a more complicated problem. Such spars, because of the shrouds that support them laterally, the stresses set up by taut wire halyards, plus headstays and backstays, are subject to tremendous compression forces. So they actually are columns that must be engineered to withstand this compression. Only a qualified designer is capable of the calculations required for the proper design of a yacht's spars.

Besides the tensile strength calculations going into mast design are the design and location of such fittings as tangs, spreaders, masthead sheaves, tracks, halyard winches, and sheet attachments. There may also be roller reefing gear to specify and suitable outhaul gear for booms. In fact the proper design of a yacht's spar plan calls for a very high degree of engineering know-how.

323. What is a mold loft? Before a yacht builder can proceed with the building of a boat, he must lay down her lines on a mold loft floor. This is a large, clean area with a smooth surface and frequently is painted white. Here the loftsmen enlarge the architect's lines, drawing to full size. From this plan the dimensions and angles of all the boat's components are transferred directly to the lumber.

When building a small boat the lines may be laid down on a sheet of plywood or even a sheet of building paper, instead of on a mold loft floor. But in any event, the lines must be laid down full size.

324. What part of a boat is the keel? This is the main backbone of the vessel to which other structural members are attached, such members as the stem, frames, deadwood, etc. On small wooden boats the keel is usually a single timber reaching from one end to the other. But on larger yachts it is sometimes necessary to scarf or joint the keel in order to produce a member long enough to fit the overall structure.

325. What is a worm shoe?   This is a piece of lumber attached to the lower surface of a wood keel to protect the latter from attacks by marine borers, such as teredos. A worm shoe is usually made from a very hard wood like oak or greenheart and is so fastened to the keel proper that it can be renewed in case of necessity.

326. What is a ballast keel?   As the term implies, this is a keel whose primary function is to provide ballast so that a boat can carry its sail. It is usually a piece of lead or iron attached outside the hull proper to the lower end of the structural keel, and its purpose is for stability.

Ballast keels also contribute to the yacht's lateral plane.

327. What is the stem of a boat?   This is the structural member at the bow of the boat to which the planking is attached. It is securely bolted or otherwise fastened to the keel and, in fact, forms a part of the boat's backbone.

328. What is meant by scarf?   When two parts of a main structural member of a yacht's hull are joined together the joint is overlapped for a considerable distance to give it strength. This overlapped joint is called a scarf.

Such a joint also is used between different members—the stem and keel, for example.

329. What does fay mean?   When two timbers are so closely joined as to be, in effect, one piece they are said to be fayed.

330. What is a faying surface?   This is the surface of a joint between two carefully fitted structural members of a vessel.

331. To what part of a boat's structure is the term "deadwood" applied?   The deadwood is the part of a boat's backbone that consists of filler pieces at the after end of the keel which is attached at the lower face of the deadwood while the horn timber is attached to the upper face.

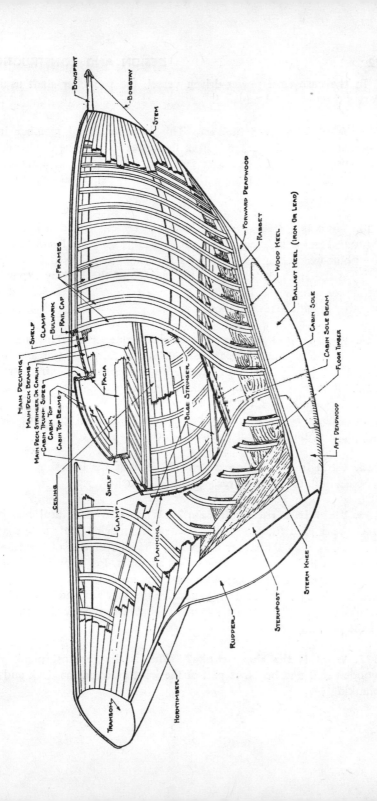

In the case of a power-driven vessel, the propeller shaft usually passes through the deadwood.

332. What is a horn timber? This is a structural member in a wooden vessel which extends from the upper face of the deadwood to the transom, and, in effect, forms a continuation of the keel and deadwood. The after end of the garboard strake is usually fastened to this member; so is the transom.

333. What is a stopwater? This is a wooden plug that is inserted through the joints between a wooden keel, stem, deadwood, etc., at the point where the planking joins these members. Its purpose is to prevent the entry of water into the interior of the hull by expanding within its transverse hole, which extends from side to side of the member in which it is installed.

334. What is the meaning of the word "transom"? This is a word that has two meanings aboard a boat. Structurally, the transom is the part of the boat's hull that extends athwartships at the extreme stern. To it the ends of the planks are attached. It forms the opposite end of the hull from the stem.

A transom is also a form of berth that can be used to form a sleeping place at night, a seat by day.

335. What is the garboard strake? This is the lowest plank on a wooden hull, the one that rests against the keel.

336. What is a rabbet (rebate)? When two structural members must be joined longitudinally, with a watertight joint, a V-shaped groove is cut in the larger into which the side or end of the smaller member will fit. This groove is called a rabbet. For example, a rabbet is cut in each side of a keel to receive the lower edge of the garboard strake. The stem is rabbeted to receive the forward ends of the hull's planking. Sometimes the transom is rabbeted to receive the after ends of the planking.

337. What is the sheer strake? This is the topmost plank of a wooden hull and becomes part of the joint between the deck and the planking.

338. What is the meaning of the word "strake"? This as a nautical term used to describe a plank as applied to the building of a vessel's hull.

339. What is a shutter (or shutter plank)? This is the name given the last plank to be applied to the hull of the vessel. Customarily, planking is applied in two sections: one section begins at the keel and works up toward the turn of the bilge; the other section commences at the sheer and works down. As the two approach each other there is left the width of a single plank between them. Into this space is fitted the shutter.

340. What is the shutter plank ceremony? This is the time when the final plank to enclose a new hull goes into place. On this occasion, it is traditional for the owner of the boat to give a party for the workmen who are building it.

341. What is caulking? As a verb, this term describes the act of filling the open seams of a vessel's planking, deck, or other parts, to render them watertight.

As a noun, it refers to the material used to render such seams tight.

342. What is a deck? This is the structural part of a vessel that encloses its upper surface and might be compared to the flat roof of a house. Customarily, on wooden vessels the deck planking runs fore and aft, parallel either to the center line or to the sheer strake. The individual planks are fastened to the deck beams, which lie below them, and the space between each plank has to be caulked to render the deck watertight. Planking of this kind should be fairly thick in order to be sufficiently strong and also to provide sufficient space for the caulking to be effective. This type of construction is called laid decking and is usually screw-fastened to the beams and the screw heads covered with wood plugs (called bungs) which match the wood of the deck.

More recent practice, particularly on medium-size and small yachts, consists in laying one or two layers of marine plywood over the deck beams and then covering them with fiber-glass cloth laid in polyester resin. This makes a very strong and tight deck and has many advantages over the older type of construction described.

On fiber-glass yachts, in order to attain the necessary rigidity that a deck requires, it is not unusual to form the deck from a cored or sandwich construction, i.e., a center core, perhaps one inch thick, made either of a foam material such as Styrofoam or balsa wood, faced on both sides with layers of fiber glass laid in polyester resin. This makes a very strong, light, and rigid watertight structure.

343. What part of a yacht is the sole?   The floor of a cabin or a cockpit is referred to as its sole.

344. What is a floor?   Contrary to what one would expect this is not something to walk on—that is called the sole. A floor is a heavy structural member that lies athwartships of the keel and joins together the lower ends of the two parts of a frame. The floor lies alongside the frame and is bolted to it and also to the keel.

345. What is a king plank?   On vessels with laid decks it is customary to have a wide plank on the center line of the deck into which the ends of the deck planking, laid parallel to the covering board, are notched and in which there is a hole for the mast or masts of a sailing yacht. Also, at its forward end the king plank will support the mooring cleat or other device used for anchoring the vessel. Customarily, the king plank is of a different material from the deck planking, usually mahogany, teak, or oak.

346. What is the covering board?   This is the structural member in a planked vessel that runs fore and aft at the edge of the deck and forms a joint between the latter and the sheer strake. The covering board usually extends out to the outside edge of the yacht's planking, thus protecting the upper edge of the sheer strake, forming a joint that can be caulked between these two parts to render them watertight. As a covering board has considerable curvature from one end to the other, it is not unusual that it should be made in a number of pieces that have to be sawed to the desired shape. All the joints, of course, must be made watertight. Customarily, such members are either mahogany, teak, or oak.

347. How are knees used in boatbuilding?   A knee is a structural member used to give additional strength to the hull and is installed wherever such strength is needed. For example, there is usually a knee between the horn timber and the transom, between the transom and the clamp, and also in the way of the mast where both hanging and lodging knees are usually used in wooden vessels.

A hanging knee is one that is installed in a more or less vertical position, and a lodging knee is one lying in a horizontal plane. Often, around the mast of a vessel there will be several of both types.

Knees are also used to strengthen the structure of the cabin house and, in fact, wherever such strength members are required.

348. What is a breasthook? This is a form of knee used at the extreme forward end of the hull where the stem and the sheer strake join.

349. What is a hackmatack knee? This is a form of natural crook that has been used for a great many years to form the breasthook or knee where the stem and the two sheer strakes of a hull join. Such knees are obtained from certain trees of the tamarack variety which grow chiefly in New England and the Great Lakes area. It is closely related to western larch.

350. What is a stringer? This is a fairly heavy structural member that extends fore and aft in the hull of a vessel. It is customarily fastened securely to the inside of the frames at the turn of the bilge (bilge stringer). In larger vessels there may be more than one stringer on each side.

351. What structural member is called a shelf? This is the heavy timber that lies horizontally inside the joint between the frames and the deck beams and to which both of these members are securely fastened. The use of such member is usually confined to larger vessels.

352. What structural member is called a clamp? This is a fore-and-aft structural member extending from stem to stern (transom) and is customarily bolted inside of the frames just low enough so the deck beams can rest on its upper surface. It is a fairly heavy timber and adds great strength to the vessel's structure.

353. What are frames? These are the two-part athwartships structural members (sometimes, in small boats, called ribs) that give the vessel her form. Frames are securely fastened to the keel at their lower end and to the clamp at their upper end and serve the purpose of holding the planking. At the turn of the bilge most boats have a bilge stringer which also lies inside the frames and adds great strength.

Frames are fairly closely spaced but do not come in contact with one another. Customarily, there is eight or ten inches or more between frames, depending upon the size of the vessel. In larger boats the spacing may be as much as a foot or more.

There are three kinds of frames used in round-bottom boats. There is the sawed frame, a heavy member that is given its shape by being cut on a bandsaw to the desired form. Often these are cut from natural crooks if such can be found. Frequently, in larger vessels, sawed frames have to be made up in more than one piece. If so, the individual pieces are called futtocks.

Another form of frame is made from steamed oak. When oak is steamed for a certain length of time it becomes very flexible and can be bent to the desired shape while still in its flexible condition.

A third form of frame is a modern development and consists of using thin strips of wood glued together with a waterproof glue. These frames are formed by clamping the laminations together over a form. In order to be sure that both sides of the boat will be the same it is good practice to laminate the members for the individual frames wide enough so they can be split down the center, thus giving two frames (one for each side) which are identical.

Usually laminated frames are made of either oak or Philippine mahogany, but other woods also—particularly those imported from the Orient—make good frame stock.

354. What are limbers? Limbers are the openings under the frames, alongside the keel, to allow bilge water to drain to the lowest part of the bilge.

355. What is a vessel's planking? As the name implies, this is the skin of the vessel which is formed by planks securely fastened to the frames, stem, keel, and other structural members with which the planking comes in contact.

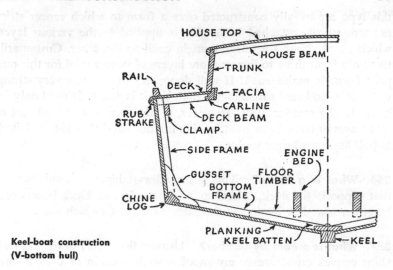

HOUSE TOP
HOUSE BEAM
TRUNK
RAIL
DECK
FACIA
CARLINE
RUB
STRAKE
DECK BEAM
CLAMP
SIDE FRAME
ENGINE BED
GUSSET
FLOOR TIMBER
BOTTOM
FRAME
CHINE LOG
PLANKING
KEEL BATTEN
KEEL

Keel-boat construction
(V-bottom hull)

Planking may be either single or double. Individual planks are called strakes and customarily run fore and aft, more or less parallel to the sheer of the vessel, except the garboard strake which has to be fitted into the rabbet of the keel, stem, etc. However, the upper edge of the garboard strake has to be formed so as to make a fair joint with the adjacent plank.

In double planking, sometimes the inner layer is laid diagonal to the frames and is of a relatively soft wood such as cedar or redwood while the outer layer runs fore and aft and may be of mahogany, cedar, or other suitable boat wood. Often in double-planked construction a layer of fabric is put between the two layers of planking in order to render them perfectly watertight. This fabric is usually laid in either shellac, white lead, paint, or a neoprene compound.

In boats of simple form—those which have no compound curves —marine plywood is frequently used in place of conventional planking. This material comes in large sheets and has certain advantages and disadvantages as compared with the older planking methods. It must be very carefully protected against moisture getting into its inner layers; otherwise it may develop rot.

Another form of planking is called molded plywood. This is suitable for use on round-bottom boats with compound curves. Boats of

78   DESIGN AND CONSTRUCTION

this type are usually constructed over a form to which veneer strips
are temporarily attached while glue is applied to the various layers
which lie at about a 90-degree angle each to the other. Customarily
there are from three to five or more layers of veneer used for this purpose (usually mahogany). If well done, this produces a very strong,
watertight, and easily maintained hull, but it is generally used only for
boats in the smaller sizes. However, a few yachts up to 40 feet or
more overall have been built by this method, and it might lend itself
to building even larger yachts.

356. What is a beam?   This is an athwartship structural member
that supports the deck, cabin top, cockpit sole, etc. Deck beams may
be either sawed or laminated the same as frames (which see).

357. What is meant by camber?   Usually this refers to the athwartships convex curvature or crown of a yacht's cabin or deck beams,
which are not straight.

The curvature in a fore-and-aft direction of a yacht's sails, when
filled with wind, is also called camber.

358. What is tumblehome?   This is a term used to describe the
gradual inward curve of a yacht's topsides from the turn of her bilge
to the deck line. Many modern designs have no tumblehome, since
lack of it tends to increase the stability of a vessel.

359. What is meant by the term "crown"?   See camber.

360. What are carlines?   These are fore-and-aft structural members
in the way of a hatch, a cockpit, or a deckhouse opening. Customarily
they are firmly secured to beams at their extremities, usually by being
dovetailed or notched into the beam, which should be an extra heavy
one to accept this joint. They are also called carlings.

361. What area of a yacht is the cabin?   This term includes all the
living space below decks except the toilet room and the engine room.
Where there is more than one cabin under a single deckhouse they are
usually designated as the forward cabin and the main cabin or saloon.
Some yachts have two separate cabins—one forward, called the main

cabin and one aft, called the after cabin. There is usually living space for two persons in the latter.

362. What is a deckhouse? On yachts this term indicates the structure above the deck that encloses the cabin or living space.

363. What is a coaming? To keep out water it is usual to surround deck openings, such as hatches and cockpits, with a vertical enclosure called a coaming. In the case of a hatch this may be only two or three inches high, but the coaming around a cockpit, which usually serves also as a backrest, will be from 3 to 10 inches or more in height. Cockpit coamings on sailboats usually run along the sides of the cockpit only, the after side being unprotected.

364. What is a hatch? An opening in the deck, or other horizontal surface, of a vessel is called a hatch or hatchway. Usually, a hatch is surrounded by a low coaming and covered with a watertight hatch cover. Sometimes a hatch cover is let in flush with the surrounding surface and has no coaming. This is called a flush hatch. This type hatch is usually made of metal but may be of any suitable material.

Where light is required below decks, hatches are often covered with Plexiglass, Lucite, or its plastic equivalent, instead of wood.

The entry to a cabin is called the companionway. The cover that slides over it is called the companion hatch or the companion slide.

365. What is a locker? In a house a locker would be called a closet or a cupboard, depending on its size. Aboard a boat a locker is a storage place, usually with a door. It is also called a hanging locker if it is intended for hanging up clothing. An oilskin locker is for hanging foul-weather clothing and often has a grating or drain in its bottom to allow water to run away into the bilge.

366. What is a cockpit? This is a depressed area in a yacht's deck, usually from knee- to waist-deep, where the crew and guests customarily spend most of their time when on deck. The cockpit sole (or floor) is usually finished in the same way as the vessel's deck.

For safety's sake cockpits are usually made self-draining so that if water gets in it will run out on its own accord. This means that the cockpit sole must be above the waterline so that the water can drain by gravity. In some boats, however, the cockpit sole is be-low the waterline, and in that case the water that accumulates in the cockpit drains into the boat's bilge, from which it must be pumped. Cockpits of the latter variety are not considered as safe as a self-bailing installation.

367. What is the purpose of a scupper?   Wherever on a boat's deck or cockpit water tends to accumulate it is customary to provide a drain. Such drains are called scuppers.

368. What is a rudder?   All sail and power boats, except outboards and outdrives, are equipped with a movable member or vane which is used to control their direction. In other words, this is the part that steers the boat.

369. What is a rudder port?   This is the name of the opening in a boat's hull through which the rudder stock enters.

370. What is a rudder stock?   This is the shaft on which a rudder pivots.

371. What part of a boat is the skeg?   On boats where the rudder is not rigged directly to the after side of the keel (as it is on a conven-tional keel sailboat) there is often a narrow fore-and-aft member on the center line near the stern just forward of the rudder. The latter is usually hinged to the skeg which strengthens and protects it from damage. A skeg also provides a modicum of lateral plane and direc-tional stability. Skegs are usually triangular, or roughly so, in shape.

On rowboats without rudders the skeg is a triangular fin away aft on the centerline to provide directional stability so it will row and tow straight.

372. What is a toe rail?   This is a low bulwark along the outer edge of a yacht's deck to prevent people or loose gear from falling over-board.

373. What is a handrail?   This is, as the name implies, a rail to be gripped by people passing along the deck. Handrails on sail-boats are usually on top of the cabin house. On powerboats they may be on the top or the side of the cabin, depending on how high the house is.

374. What is a liferail?   It is customary to provide wire safety lines —sometimes single, sometimes double—along the rail of a yacht to keep the crew and guests from falling overboard. The wire is usually covered with white plastic material and is supported at appropriate intervals by metal stanchions, bolted to the deck or the covering board.

Frequently there is an opening in the liferail on the starboard side to permit people to board the vessel without having to climb over it. This opening is closed when all are aboard.

375. What is a pulpit?   This is the structure or fitting at the bow of a yacht, either sail or power, made from stainless steel tubing, to which the lifelines are attached. Some yachts also have a pulpit at the stern as well.

376. What are topsides?   This is the area of a yacht's hull between the rail and the waterline.

377. What is the boot top?   This is the name of the narrow band of contrasting paint which, on some yachts, appears between the topside and bottom paints. It is purely decorative.

378. What is a sump?   The lowest part of a boat's bilge is called the sump. It is here that the bilge pump is usually located.

If a yacht has a shower it usually drains into a special receptacle which is called a sump. This term can be applied to any container used to receive drainage in a boat.

379. What is a centerboard?   This is a wooden board or a metal plate which is adjustable up and down. It is usually pivoted at its forward end and is adjusted by means of a pendant at its after end. It fits inside a centerboard trunk on the boat's keel and provides lateral resistance to a sailboat.

380. Of what materials are centerboards made?   Centerboards can be made of wood, metal or fiber glass, sometimes a combination of these materials.

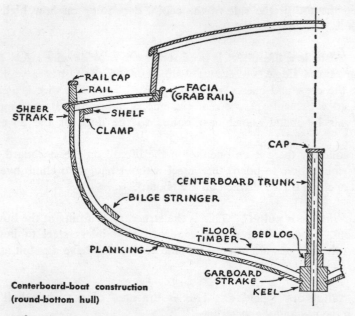

Centerboard-boat construction
(round-bottom hull)

381. What is a centerboard trunk? In its simplest form a centerboard trunk is simply a watertight slot, open at top and bottom, in which the centerboard is a loose fit. Its lower end is securely fastened to the keel and is open to the water beneath.

In some boats the top opening is closed with a cover. In big centerboard yachts (usually ocean racers) the centerboard trunk is often built of welded bronze or steel.

382. What is a centerboard pendant? This is the name given the rope that is used to adjust a centerboard. It is usually attached at or near the after end of the board and leads up through the top of the centerboard trunk to a cleat where is is made fast. In larger boats with heavy centerboards, the pendant is stainless steel rope and is led over sheaves to a geared winch or reel on which it is wound by hand.

There are some one-design classes where the centerboard pendant leads forward and either is a tackle or leads to a specially designed offset winch.

383. What is an offset centerboard winch? This is a hoisting device which has two drums—one large, one small in diameter. The centerboard pendant is taken up on the small drum when a lanyard, wrapped around the large drum, is pulled. This provides leverage to make it easier to raise the centerboard.

384. Does a centerboard give stability to a boat? No. A centerboard does not contribute stability unless heavily weighted.

385. What are twin centerboards? These are the same as a single centerboard, except that they are arranged in tandem—the main board forward, the mizzen board aft. Usually the mizzen board is somewhat smaller than the main board. This arrangement, although costly to install, has several advantages. Principally, they permit a very accurate adjustment of a vessel's center of lateral resistance (CLR) in relation to the center of effort (CE) of its sails. By adjusting these centers correctly a vessel can be made to hold its course for long periods without being steered by its rudder, a great advantage for long-distance cruises. Twin centerboards are not used on small boats and seldom on racing yachts.

386. What are bilgeboards? These are similar to centerboards, except that there are two on a boat instead of one. They are parallel to the keel and are located side by side, well away from each other. They have certain advantages, as they leave a clear space in the cockpit and, being set at a slight angle from the vertical, are more effective when the boat heels over in a breeze. Bilgeboards are used mostly on inland lake scows, which are very fast racing boats. As each board requires a trunk, they cost more to install than a centerboard.

387. What are leeboards? These serve to provide lateral resistance, like a centerboard. They are carried outside the hull, secured to the topsides near the rail, and can be raised or lowered. They are seldom used in the United States except on sailing canoes. They are familiar features of Dutch sailboats, however.

388. What is a dagger board? A dagger board serves the same purpose as a centerboard. The difference is that it is not pivoted at its forward end, but is raised and lowered directly and held in place by a pin inserted through the trunk and board. Dagger boards are usually used only on small boats.

389. What are bilge keels on a sailboat? On a sailboat they are smaller substitutes for a conventional center-line keel. Bilge keels are located some distance from the hull's center line, and there are always two of them, one on each side.

390. On a powerboat, what are bilge keels? Ordinarily, powerboats don't have bilge keels, but they are sometimes installed on boats that have a tendency to roll excessively. They are intended to reduce rolling and are attached to the hull in a fore-and-aft direction, more or less parallel to the main keel, and are long shallow members. They do not provide ballast and almost inevitably subtract something from a boat's speed.

391. What is a weldment? This is a term used to describe a metal fitting made up from structural shapes, such as plates or angles, which are welded together to form a unit.

In modern ocean racing yachts weldments are frequently used for mast steps, centerboard trunks, and engine beds.

392. What is an engine bed? All engines have to be mounted on a firm foundation and securely bolted down. The structure on which they are mounted is called an engine bed. It can be of wood (usually oak) or a metal weldment. The bed is, of course, securely bolted to the hull of the boat so as to provide a firm foundation for the engine.

393. Of what materials are boats built? From the earliest days, wood has been the material from which boats were built. After the development of waterproof glues it became possible to build boats of plywood, which has the advantage of being light in weight and having no seams. Pleasure boats have also been built of steel for many years, and more recently aluminum is gaining in popularity for boatbuilding.

The biggest change in boatbuilding materials, however, has come with the development of fiber glass. This material, if properly fabricated, makes a hull that is smooth, strong, leakproof, and needs little maintenance.

Other plastic materials have been tried from time to time, but fiber glass is by far the most popular.

394. What woods are suitable for boatbuilding? The wood that goes into a boat varies according to its purpose. The backbone (stem, keel, deadwood, etc.) will be one wood, frames or ribs may be of another, planking of a third, deck of a fourth, and trim of a fifth wood. If a boat has wooden spars, they will be of still another variety. In different sections of the country different woods are frequently used. Certain components (stems, keels, frames, deck beams, for example) may be laminated; that is, they may be of strips glued together. This is regarded as superior construction.

Here is a partial table of the most popular woods and the purposes for which they are used:

	keels, stems, etc.	frames and deck beams	stringers	decks	trim	planking	spars
white oak	x	x					
yellow pine	x		x			x	
mahogany	x	x			x	x	
teak				x	x	x	
white cedar						x	
Sitka spruce							x
fir		x					
marine plywood				x		x	
Alaska cedar						x	
white pine				x			
Port Orford cedar						x	
cypress						x	

395. What are the eight principal methods of planking a boat? Carvel, lapstrake (clinker), strip (glued seam), batten seam, double planking, cross planking, sheet plywood, and molded plywood.

396. What is carvel planking? It is the planking method in which the planks are laid edge to edge, having a flush surface both inside and out. The seam is usually caulked to prevent leakage. Planks taper from the middle toward each end.

397. What is lapstrak planking? Another name for this type of planking is "clinker." In this type of construction the lower part of an upper plank laps over the top of its neighbor below. Such overlaps, or seams, are usually riveted to make a tight joint. The final result is strong for its weight but is sometimes difficult to keep watertight. In newer hulls the overlaps are usually glued as well as riveted. This method of planking is used for certain dinghies, sea skiffs, and some outboards. Clinker planking tapers fore and aft, like carvel planking.

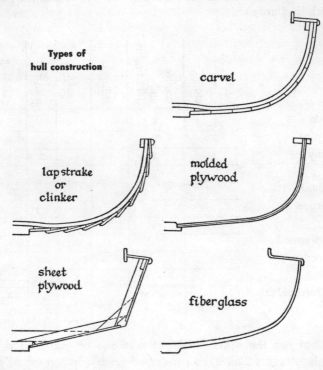

Types of
hull construction

carvel

lapstrake
or
clinker

molded
plywood

sheet
plywood

fiberglass

398. What is strip planking? This is also called glued seam construction. Planks are approximately square in section and do not taper longitudinally as they usually do in other planking methods. This makes for easy and cheap building. Glue is applied to all seams, and nails are driven through planks from above, usually penetrating two and a half planks. If well done, this is very strong and tight construction. It needs fewer internal frames than carvel or clinker planking and is smooth on both sides.

There is, however, a negative side to this planking method. With modern resorcinol glues, which are actually stronger than the wood, the planked skin of the boat becomes, to all intents, a single unit. All woods, some more than others, tend to shrink across the grain when dry and to swell when wet. The planking of a glued hull is practically one wide plank, perhaps as wide as 15 feet or more. When a plank this wide (if there were such a thing) shrinks, it sets up tremendous stresses in its internal structure, tending to cause a pulling apart, or splitting, of the wood. As the glued joints are so strong the splits occur in the wood itself, between the glue lines. Such splits can cause leaks to develop. On a normally planked boat such leaks would be recaulked to stop the leak, but this isn't practical on glued strip construction, as forcing caulking into a split would only cause it to split further. Repairing such splits takes the best efforts of a good boatbuilder. Fortunately it is possible, however.

399. What is batten seam construction?   In this method the planks are laid much as in carvel construction but a batten, to which the planks are riveted (and sometimes glued), is laid behind each seam. This makes for light, strong, and tight construction, requiring fewer frames than the carvel or clinker type. Batten seam construction is mostly used in powerboats.

400. What is double planking?   As the name implies, this is a method in which one layer of planking is laid over another. Sometimes the inner planking is laid diagonally; the outer planks run fore-and-aft as in carvel construction. A layer of fabric, suitably impregnated, is usually laid between the two layers of planks to render them watertight.

The inner planking is usually a soft, light wood such as cedar or redwood. The outer planking is generally a harder wood such as mahogany. This type planking is seldom found in small boats. Double planking does not usually require its seams to be caulked.

401. What is cross planking?   The bottom of most flat-bottom skiffs has planks laid from side to side and nailed to the lower edges of the boat's sides. Seams have to be caulked to keep them tight.

In certain areas, such as Chesapeake Bay, a variation of the cross planking to suit V-bottom boats has been developed. This planking is usually laid diagonally from the keel to the boat's sides.

402. What is sheet plywood planking?   As the name implies, this is a planking method using marine grade sheet plywood over a conventional wooden frame. It is suitable only for hulls with chines, so the topsides are one or more sheets of plywood per side. They meet the bottom planking at the chine. As it is practically impossible to put a compound curve into sheet plywood, hulls of this type are relatively simple in form, usually being of flat, V, or arc bottom conformation.

403. What is molded plywood planking?   This is a type of construction that is used in building round-bottom boats, such as 14-foot dinghies, Thistles, etc. To build such a hull it is first necessary to construct a form or mold over which the planking is laid. Such hulls are usually covered with several layers of veneer strips about one-sixteenth inch thick and four to five inches wide. These are laid diagonally, each layer crossing the one beneath at about a 90-degree angle. Glue is applied between each layer, and staples are used to hold the veneer in place until the glue sets. The staples may or may not be removed after the hull is completed. If they are not rustproof, they may cause rust stains on the hull.

This type hull is light, strong, and smooth both inside and out. Frames or ribs are not needed, but knees are usually installed alongside the centerboard trunk to lend support for the stresses set up there when under sail.

Unless the top edges of the planking are well protected with paint or varnish, there is a possibility that fresh water may work its way into any voids between the strips. This can cause dry rot in the inner layers.

404. Can plywood boats, either sheet or molded, be repaired if damaged?   Yes, quite easily, by cutting out damaged areas and fitting in new wood of the same kind, which is glued in position.

405. What kind of glue is used in boatbuilding?   Waterproof glue. The most popular variety goes under the generic term resorcinol. This type glue is made by several manufacturers. Perhaps the best known brand is Elmer's Waterproof, made by the Borden Company.

Resorcinal glue is a two-component mixture that sets by chemical reaction, not by evaporation, as do the old type glues.

406. What is fiber glass? This is a new structural material that is basically glass fiber and resin. The glass can be in the form of mat, cloth, or roving. The resin is usually polyester or epoxy.

Both materials are made by many manufacturers, but the pioneer and principal producer of the glass compound is the Owens-Corning Fiberglas Corporation. The resins are made by several chemical companies under various trade names.

407. How long has fiber glass been in use? It was developed during World War II at Wright Field, Dayton, Ohio, by the U.S. Air Force for making strong airplane components.

408. When was fiber glass adapted to boatbuilding? Soon after World War II the first fiber-glass boats were produced.

409. How are fiber-glass boats built? First a full-size model of the boat is very carefully built, usually of wood. Its surface has to be exceptionally smooth, as any irregularities would show up on the finished boat. This model, called a plug, is then covered with a parting agent (usually cellophane) to prevent the plastic from sticking to it.

Fiberglass and plastic are applied to the plug to form a female mold. For small boats this mold may be in one piece, but for big ones it usually is in two halves.

When the plastic-glass form or mold has set it is removed from the plug and used as a mold to form fiber-glass boats.

The two halves of the mold are joined. The very smooth inside surface is covered with a parting agent (usually a form of wax) to prevent adhesion. Working inside the mold, workers apply fiber glass and plastic to a suitable thickness. When this has set, the mold is parted and the boat's hull is removed.

The plug is preserved, as it can be used to form many molds. The molds are good for forming only a limited number of boats. They have to be replaced periodically due to wear and tear.

410. What are the principal advantages of fiber glass as a boat-building material? It is strong. The exterior of a component, such as a hull or cabin, is perfectly smooth. Color can be impregnated at the time of molding. If properly built a fiber-glass boat should be leak-proof. Being molded material, it permits the yacht designer greater latitude in developing a hull form than any other boatbuilding material. It requires almost no upkeep, at least for the first few years. Marine organisms such as teredos, will not attack it, but barnacles and other marine growths will adhere to the bottom of a fiber-glass boat that is not protected with an antifouling paint.

411. What are the disadvantages of fiber glass? The inner surfaces of fiber-glass boats are usually rough, so they are hard to keep clean. If the materials from which the boat is molded are improperly mixed, it may result in a porous hull which will allow water to seep in continually. If a fiber-glass boat's topsides get fouled with oil, it can be difficult or impossible to clean them. Adding fixtures or fittings is more difficult than on a wooden boat, as it requires the use of glass and resin and metalworking tools, the material being too hard for woodworking tools. The decks of small fiber-glass boats tend to be springy under a person's weight. They are also very slippery when wet unless they have a well-textured surface.

412. Can damaged fiber-glass boats be repaired? Yes, quite easily Even very extensive damage can be repaired so the hull is restored to perfect condition.

413. What maintenance does a fiber-glass boat require? For the first few years a fiber-glass boat will only need to be washed off, and its bottom coated with antifouling paint, to keep it in good condition. In time, however, the condition of the fiber-glass surfaces exposed to weathering begins to deteriorate somewhat. It then becomes necessary to paint these surfaces in order to keep up the boat's appearance.

414. Can wood and fiber-glass be used together in new construction? Yes. Wood boats can be covered on the outside with fiber glass, which will then provide many of the advantages of the latter material. Some steel boats have also been successfully covered with fiber glass.

415. What are the principal disadvantages of steel boats? The disadvantages of steel boats include rusting if the steel is not properly protected, sweating inside unless suitably insulated, and a tendency to transmit exterior temperature to the interior. The latter, in a cold climate, can be quite uncomfortable.

Welded steel hulls, unless expertly built, tend to have an irregular surface which can be faired by the application of fairing compound. If the compound scales off, it leaves unsightly blemishes on the hull. To prevent rust spots a steel vessel needs frequent painting. Care must be used to prevent electrolysis in a steel hull.

416. What are the principal advantages of steel boats? They are strong and, if well-built, they don't leak. If damaged they are easily repaired. It is easy, by welding, to attach components such as a chain plate or other fittings. Steel boats are impervious to attack by marine borers.

417. Does aluminum make a satisfactory boat? Yes, if the right alloy is used and if the hull is properly fabricated. Until recently aluminum could not be welded satisfactorily, and hulls were riveted. This was slow and costly. Welding has revolutionized the building of aluminum boats, and hulls are now built in almost all sizes from the smallest to the largest.

Except for rusting, an aluminum hull is subject to the same general advantages and disadvantages as one of steel. Great care must be taken in all metal hulls to prevent electrolysis due to using incompatible metals below the waterline or to the improper installation of electrical equipment such as telephones, etc.

418. Are building kits available? Yes, there are numerous manufacturers offering kits in various stages of completion for the amateur builder. Most of these are smaller boats, but boats up to 50 feet are also available in this form.

419. How much can be saved by building a kit boat? Generally speaking, about 40 percent of the cost of building a boat is in the materials. Therefore, up to 60 percent can be saved if a boat is kit-built.

420. Why are boats christened by breaking a bottle of champagne over the bow? In ancient times it was customary to offer human sacrifices at the launching of a new vessel. Eventually, this custom was modified to the offering of animal sacrifice. Then, as men became a little more civilized, various forms of offering to the sea god were used, but the shedding of blood, either human or animal, was abandoned. The modern custom of breaking a bottle of champagne over the new vessel's bow as she is christened and launched is the direct descendant of these old rites.

VII. FITTINGS

Introduction. Marine hardware is a highly specialized feature of boating to which countless men have devoted endless hours of thought and development. For nearly every task aboard every type of boat imaginable there is some sort of specialized fitting that makes a particular function possible. If just the right fitting is not available, or the one at hand seems to be lacking in some regard, the yachtsman will, more often than not, go to work inventing the necessary part or improving upon the one that already exists. By nature, sailors are great gadgeteers and are constantly reaching for a perfection in fittings that is, seemingly, never quite attainable. Advancing technology, which in some cases had its development for other applications in different fields, has had a marked effect in recent years upon yachting gear and fittings.

421. What is a winch? A winch is a mechanical device consisting of a base, a rotating barrel or drum, which turns only in one direction, and a portable handle used to turn the barrel.

422. For what purpose is a winch used? Winches are used on yachts to gain the mechanical advantage necessary to hoist sails and to trim their sheets.

423. What is a reel winch? This winch is normally used on wire main halyards of larger boats. The entire halyard is wire and it is wound around the winch drum as the sail is hoisted, so that there is nothing left to coil.

424. What is a snubbing winch? A snubbing winch has no handle and is used on small boats to provide mechanical advantage for holding a sheet and trimming it.

425. What is a winch handle? A winch handle is the lever by means of which most winches are operated.

93

426. Are winch handles removable?   Most winch handles may be detached from their winches, but there are smaller types that are integrally mounted. Removable winch handles have a way of slipping overboard, so it is well to have some secure means of stowing them.

427. Are electrical winches allowed on racing yachts?   No. The racing rules allow only mechanical winches that are powered by human muscle.

428. What is a jig?   Before the advent of winches the only way the mechanical advantage necessary to handle large sails could be gained was by the use, on halyards and sheets, of tackles which were called jigs.

429. How was a jig rigged?   Where a jig was required to hoist or trim a sail the halyard (for hoisting) or the sheet (for trimming) was usually double-ended with the jig permanently attached to one end only. The free end of the halyard or sheet would be hauled by main strength until the strain became too great. That end was then secured, or made fast, and the last few feet of movement were gained by transferring the effort to the jig which was attached to the other end. The advantage gained depended, of course, on the number of parts in the jig or tackle. (See tackles.)

430. Is it possible to use a jig on a single-part wire?   Yes, but special blocks are required: one a snatch block with a becket at each end to be spliced into the standing part and the second being a fixed opensided deck block, essentially a second snatch block.

Such a rig would not be necessary if there were a jig downhaul at the gooseneck.

431. How is a jig on a single-part wire halyard rigged?   The haul end of the wire is eye-spliced into the upper becket of a two-becket snatch block. To the lower becket of the same block a manila or Dacron hauling part is eye-spliced. This piece of rope has to be long enough to reach from the halyard cleat to the masthead, and the wire part must be long enough to reach from the headboard of the sail, when lowered, to the forward side of the masthead halyard sheave.

432. What is the method of hoisting a sail with a jig on a single-part halyard? Haul away by hand on the rope halyard until the sail is almost mastheaded. Then pass the rope part through the fixed deck block and lead it back over the sheave of the snatch block. Finally, belay the rope part to the cleat on the mast, which should be located two or three feet below the snatch block.

433. What is a coffee grinder? This is a slang expression applied to the big two-handled winches used on large racing yachts to trim the sheets of Genoa jibs and spinnakers which are so big that it is impossible to develop the necessary power for sheet trimming by any other means.

434. What is a block? This is the nautical term for what a landsman calls a pulley. It consists of a body or shell, with a pin through its middle on which a sheave (or sheaves) is free to rotate. A block with one sheave is called a single block, with two sheaves a double block, and so on.

There are a great many blocks for special services, and they are designated according to their purpose or their construction. Some yacht blocks have wood shells (usually ash or lignum vitae), some have bronze or stainless steel shells, and some of the more recent type have shells made from certain very strong plastics.

435. What is a fair-lead? A fair-lead, as its name implies, is simply a means of leading a piece of running rigging through or around an obstruction so that the chances of its becoming fouled or worn are reduced to a minimum.

436. What is a sheave? A sheave is a small grooved metal wheel or pulley, usually contained between the cheeks of a block, where it is free to rotate on a pin or axle. Yacht blocks often have sheaves with roller bushings instead of plain bearings. Such bushings make the sheave run a lot easier and so multiply the block's efficiency.

Certain sheaves, such as those for masthead halyards, rotate in fixed positions. Such sheaves sometimes have special grooves made to accommodate both wire and rope running rigging.

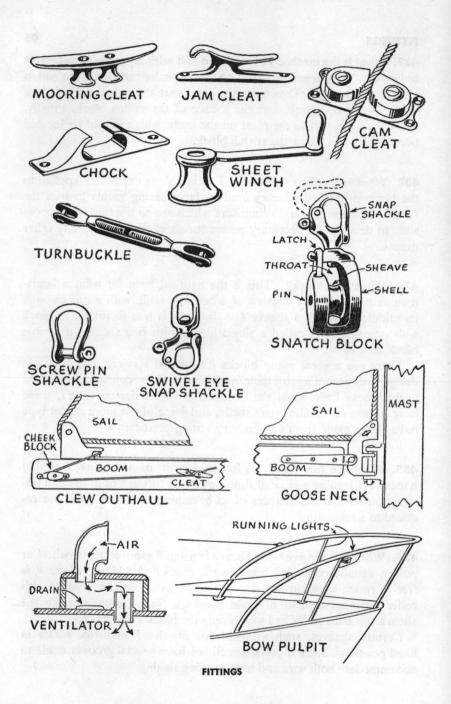

MOORING CLEAT

JAM CLEAT

CAM CLEAT

CHOCK

SHEET WINCH

TURNBUCKLE

SNAP SHACKLE

LATCH

THROAT

SHEAVE

PIN

SHELL

SNATCH BLOCK

SCREW PIN SHACKLE

SWIVEL EYE SNAP SHACKLE

CHEEK BLOCK

SAIL

BOOM

CLEAT

CLEW OUTHAUL

SAIL

MAST

BOOM

GOOSE NECK

RUNNING LIGHTS

AIR

DRAIN

VENTILATOR

BOW PULPIT

FITTINGS

437. What is a cleat?   This is a fitting, made of metal or wood, used to secure (belay) a line. Cleats take many forms depending on their intended use.

438. What is a jam cleat?   This is a cleat that holds the line by squeezing it so it is not necessary to belay it. They are used mostly to secure sheets, as they permit quick release.

439. What is a pin rail?   This is a permanent, usually U-shaped rail, located on deck at the foot of a mast in which belaying pins are fitted for making fast, or belaying, halyards, lifts, etc. A pin rail is usually supported at a convenient height by four turned wood stanchions, or legs. Pin rails have been used for centuries, but they are not found on most modern yachts, whose sails are hoisted with winches and wire halyards.

440. What is a gooseneck?   The gooseneck is a metal boom-end fitting by means of which a boom is attached to a mast. It is essentially a universal joint.

441. What is a boom jack?   A boom jack is a specialized piece of equipment, found only on larger sailboats, that takes the place of a boom downhaul. It is a mechanical means of lowering the boom and is usually operated with a ratchet lever.

442. What is a boom crutch?   This is a removable crutchlike device that is used to support the outboard end of a boom in a horizontal position when sails are not set. A topping lift may also be used for this purpose.

443. What is a gallows frame?   Gallows frames used to be much more common than they are today on cruising yachts. They are basically permanent boom crutches and are particularly useful for supporting the boom when tying in a reef.

444. What is a mainsheet traveler?   This is a slide, track or rail to which is attached the lower part of the mainsheet. It allows the on-deck part (or parts) of the sheet to move from side to side according to what tack the boat is on. The trim of a sail can often be improved by adjustments to the traveler.

445. What is a tabernacle?   A tabernacle is a fitting into which a mast is stepped on deck. It allows the mast to be lowered by releasing the headstay and, with block and tackle control, letting it fall aft. A tabernacle is particularly useful when a great many low bridges must be cleared, as it is a simple means of raising and lowering the mast.

446. What is a spinnaker pole end fitting?   A spinnaker pole end fitting normally contains a spring-loaded pin so that the pole may be attached to and released from a spinnaker clew. Points of attachment for the spinnaker pole topping lift and downhaul also are sometimes found on this fitting.

447. What is a spinnaker pole bell?   This is a cup-shaped fitting on a track at the forward side of the main or fore mast. The fitting on the end of the spinnaker pole fits inside and is held by the bell. The height of the bell on the mast of larger yachts is controlled by an uphaul and downhaul arrangement.

448. What is roller reefing?   This is a special group of fittings that are employed on the main boom of a sailboat so that the mainsail can be reefed by rolling it around the boom.

Necessary are a boom that is round, a special fitting at the gooseneck that uses a crank to turn the boom, and a swivel fitting at the outer end of the boom to which the mainsheet and topping lift are attached and within which the boom can rotate.

449. What is roller furling gear?   This equipment is found on cruising sailboats and simplifies the task of setting and taking in a jib. The sail simply rolls up on its wire luff rope when a lanyard is pulled, and is left standing in this fashion.

450. What is a backstay lever?   This lever is used to set up and release (when not in use) the running backstay on larger yachts. It eliminates the necessity of a winch for a running backstay, but means that tension on the backstay cannot be controlled as with a winch.

451. What is a capstan? On a yacht this is a piece of mechanical equipment located on the forward deck and used for getting up the anchor. It may be either hand- or power-operated by either hydraulic pressure or electricity.

452. What is a shackle? This is a U-shaped metal fitting used to make a connection between two dissimilar pieces of equipment: an anchor and an anchor rode, or a turnbuckle and a chain plate, for example. For yacht use, shackles are usually bronze, stainless steel, or galvanized, drop forged steel. A pin extends between the two arms of the U and either it terminates in a screw thread which fits into one of the arms, or it may pass through a clearance hole in the shackle and have a cotter pin in its end to hold it in position. Its opposite end usually terminates in a small eye.

453. What are chocks? These are metal leads for anchor and docking lines where they pass the boat's rail that are designed to keep chafing to a minimum.

454. What is a davit, and how is it used? In modern yachts davits are used for hoisting heavy objects, such as anchors or boats. On really big yachts they also act as supports for gangways. Modern davits are made of iron, but wooden davits were used to haul boats in whale ships. A davit is really a small derrick.

VIII. MAINTENANCE, SAFETY, LAWS AND REGULATIONS

Introduction. Outfitting and maintaining a boat in good operating condition is a never-ending task, but one that can have its rewards in the satisfaction gained from smart appearance and reliable performance. Like anything else, a boat will respond best to a constant program of preventive maintenance.

While outfitting, it is important to know of the applicable safety equipment regulations and registration requirements for a particular type of boat. These are essential to a properly outfitted vessel and are backed up by law.

455. In using a manufactured product on a boat, what rule should always be followed?   Follow the manufacturer's directions, if available. He knows best.

456. Which is generally considered the season for outfitting one's boat?   The spring is when most annual maintenance is done, even in year-round boating areas. The wise boatman, however, does as much as possible in the fall to avoid the last-minute spring rush.

457. If a boat is stored in a yard, may an owner still do his own work?   This, of course, depends upon the individual yard's policies. A general rule, often found, is that no work may be done above the deck or outside the rail by other than yard personnel.

There are some yards, however, that allow any and all work to be done by others.

458. Do fiber-glass hulls need painting every year?   No, a new fiber-glass boat should be able to go three or four years without painting, depending upon the care and quality of upkeep. Once a fiber-glass hull receives a coat of paint, however, it must be painted every year just like any other boat.

Antifouling bottom paint must be applied each year, of course.

459. What preparation should be made for antifouling paint to be applied to a new fiber-glass bottom? Be sure all traces of the wax parting agent used in manufacturing have been removed by washing with a strong detergent solution. Sand off all gloss so that the paint will have a chance to adhere properly. Follow exactly the instructions on the can.

460. What is a gel coat on a fiber-glass hull? This is the hard, glossy, outer surface that contains the color; the final finish coat.

461. How should a fiber-glass surface be cleaned? With a mild abrasive kitchen cleanser such as Bon-Ami or Babo. They will not scratch the high-gloss finish.

462. What may be used to remove stubborn marks from fiber glass? Soaped steel wool pads have been found to be effective. Care should be taken, however, not to take the gloss off the finish.

463. What is the best way to remove grease and tar from a fiber-glass surface? A common petroleum solvent such as gasoline or carbon tet can be used to remove these stains.

464. Can a fiber-glass hull be waxed? Yes, it is very much like an automobile finish and the same polishing products will do an excellent job.

465. Is it a good idea to wax fiber-glass decks and superstructures? Because traction may be impaired and light reflection increased, it is best not to wax these areas.

466. What can be done to restore a fiber-glass surface that has become dull and faded? Before going to painting, try using a fine grade abrasive cleanser or rubbing compound. There are products on the market designed especially for this purpose, and they may make painting unnecessary for some time thereafter.

467. Must a primer be used before painting a fiber-glass surface? With epoxy paint, priming is not necessary. With conventional alkydtype paints you cannot depend on good adhesion unless a prime coat is first applied.

468. Can chemical paint removers be used on fiber glass?   Yes, but care must be taken that the chemicals do not damage the gel coat. Test a small area first to see how it works. Leave the chemical on only long enough to dissolve the paint. Then wash the area with fresh water and a mild detergent to neutralize the remover's effects.

469. How can surface damage to a fiber-glass boat be repaired? If color matching is not required, a polyester putty or epoxy compound does a good job.

To match the gel coat color, it is best to obtain resin from the manufacturer, because colors are always hard to match.

470. What is indicated if the surface of a fiber-glass hull shows hairline cracks?   Usually hairline cracks go no deeper than the surface gel coat and should cause no serious concern. Unless they create an unsightly appearance, it is probably not even worth trying to repair them.

471. What is the most important consideration in maintaining an aluminum or steel hull?   Protection against corrosion, which is easy enough to provide if a meticulous maintenance program is followed.

472. How are aluminum boats finished?   They are either finished naturally or painted with a special process. This is generally not considered a job for an amateur and is best left to an experienced yard. Antifouling bottom paints should be applied each year, but great care must be exercised to make sure suitable barrier coats are applied between the hull and the antifouling (usually copper-bearing) paint. Follow the maker's recommendations to the letter.

473. Are finishes of all types made especially for marine use?   Yes. In addition to bottom paints there are numerous others made specially for boat applications. For example, deck paint, spar varnish, engine enamel, topside, and boot-top paints.

474. What is epoxy paint?   Epoxy paint comes in two parts—a base which has the color pigment added and an activating agent. The latter is poured into a half-full base can (it comes that way) and they are mixed for a prescribed period. There is a waiting period for chemical reaction to take place before the paint can be applied, and the working time is limited. Read the label.

475. What is antifouling paint? This is a paint that is applied to the bottom of a boat to prevent fouling by marine growths such as barnacles, borers, etc. Ths principal ingredient in most such paints is copper in the form of cuprous oxide, suspended in a liquid called a vehicle. It should exfoliate slowly, allowing new copper to be exposed and providing a poor surface for marine growths.

476. What is the best kind of bottom paint? Ideally, a bottom paint should be hard and smooth, and at the same time antifouling. This is a hard order to fill, but the vinyl-based, copper-bearing bottom paints have gained great popularity because they come as close as anything to meeting these requirements.

477. How soon after applying an antifouling bottom should the boat be launched? This will vary according to the paint, and the manufacturer's directions should always be followed. As a general rule, however, remember that bottom paint may lose much of its antifouling property if allowed to dry too long.

478. How is a surface prepared for painting? The entire area must be throughly sanded, taking care to remove the gloss from any old paint. Touch up with filler compound any areas that are chipped or worn. Go over these places with a paint brush and, when dry, sand lightly before painting.

479. Why should painting be avoided in the late afternoon? If the air begins to get damp before a gloss-finish paint has had a good chance to set, the end result will not be very satisfactory. You will have a finish that, if glossy at all, won't last very long.

480. When a surface gets too thick with paint what happens and what must be done? When a surface has been painted over and over the finish builds up until it reaches a point where it begins to look shabby and to peel off. It is then necessary to strip the entire surface down to the bare wood and start again.

481. What are three ways of stripping old paint off a wooden boat? (1) Sanding;   (2) chemical paint remover;   (3) burning off and scraping.

482. What is meant by the term "brightwork"?   Contrary to the way it sounds, brightwork is not highly polished hardware but the varnished wood exterior trim on a boat. It is usually either teak or mahogany, and sometimes the former is left unfinished.

483. Why is it necessary to prevent excessive build-up of varnish on brightwork?   Most varnish is brittle to start with and tends to become more so with each coat. It chips and cracks with temperature changes more easily than paint, which allows water to seep through and discolor the wood.

Also, varnish is not supposed to hide the attractive grain and color of the wood, which can happen if its gets too thick.

484. When is it necessary to recaulk a seam?   When the seam compound dries out after a period of time, it will crack with the swelling and shrinking of the planks. When its putty-like consistency is lost, it is usually time to recaulk the seam.

485. Why is it important that a boat be well ventilated below? Good ventilation keeps a boat smelling sweet and fresh. Dampness and an atmosphere that breeds mildew are not very pleasant to live with. Also, dry rot is likely to occur where air circulation is poor.

486. What is dry rot?   Wood, being of cellular structure and cut from a living tree, is subject, under certain conditions, to attack by a fungal growth which saps its strength and turns it dark. Such disintegration is mistakenly referred to as dry rot. The disease tends to spread, once it becomes established. Paradoxically, wood must have a moisture content of over 20 percent to induce so-called dry rot.

487. What causes dry rot?   It is generally accepted that dry rot is caused by the seepage of fresh water (rain and dew) into the joints and seams in a boat's structure. If this moisture accumulates in a confined space, where the free circulation of air is impossible, dry rot is likely to develop.

A boat left under a leaky tarpulin is particularly likely to develop the disease.

488. What woods are least subject to attack by dry rot?   Among woods commonly used in boatbuilding, the most rot-resistant are teak, white cedar, cypress, and redwood. The latter is too soft to make good outer planking but is sometimes used for the inner layer of a double-planked boat. Even teak, cypress and cedar may develop dry rot under particularly adverse conditions.

489. What can be done to cure dry rot?   Nothing. Once it has developed the only way to get rid of dry rot is to cut out the affected parts and put new wood in its place.

490. How does one recognize dry rot?   Wood affected by the disease usually turns dark and gets soft and spongy. If the surface is painted, the change may not be apparent to the eye, but tapping with a hammer will reveal the affected areas by the flat sound of the taps.

Sometimes, in big timbers such as oak keels, it is necessary to bore holes to determine if dry rot exists at the heart of the wood. If it is found it indicates that poorly seasoned wood was used.

491. Where is dry rot most likely to occur in a boat?   It first attacks the end grain and occurs mostly at the extreme bow and stern of decked boats, areas where air circulation may be poor. Dry rot also frequently is found behind poorly insulated iceboxes in cruising boats. In this area the cold given off will cause damp air to condense on the planking.

Open boats are seldom affected unless they were built of unseasoned wood.

492. Can dry rot be prevented?   Yes. There are preparations on the market which, if applied when the boat is built, will prevent the development of the disease in sound wood. Known generically as copper nephthenate, this product, which usually dyes the wood green, is marketed under various names, the best known marine product being Cuprinol.

Frames, planking, and other members should be treated before assembly to assure all surfaces being covered. If the wood was infected before treatment, however, such application may be ineffective.

493. How is copper nephthenate applied?   It is usually applied with a brush or spray. This treatment, however, is not very effective in preventing dry rot in big timbers such as the stem, keel, and deadwood. To preserve these, they should be immersed in a bath (preferably under pressure) of copper nephthenate until the pores of the wood are filled with the chemical.

494. How can one tell if wood has been treated to prevent dry rot? Copper nephthenate, as used in boatbuilding, gives bare wood a green color, so one can tell by inspection if it has been treated. If the surface is painted, the only way to be sure is to scrape off the paint in spots to reveal the bare wood.

495. What is electrolysis?   This is a phenomenon caused by the adjacent exposure in salt water of metals that are incompatible. A low tension electric current flows between them causing the less noble metal (see galvanic series) slowly to disintegrate.

496. What steps can be taken to prevent electrolysis from damaging underwater appendages?   The usual precaution is to install closely adjacent to, but not in contact with, the unit to be protected a zinc or magnesium plate. These metals, being at the less noble end of the galvanic series (which see), will disintegrate slowly due to galvanic action, but in so doing they divert such action from the member being protected. They must be replaced when one third is left.

497. What is the galvanic series?   This is a list of metals arranged in the order of their corrosion resistance, with the metal most subject to corrosion (called least noble) at the top and the one least subject to corrosion (most noble) at the bottom.

TABLE 1.

GALVANIC SERIES OF METALS.

CORRODED END (*anodic, or least noble*)
Magnesium
Zinc
Aluminum
Cadmium
Steel or Iron
Cast Iron
Chromium-iron (active)
Lead-tin solders
Lead
Tin
Nickel (active)
Brasses
Copper
Bronzes *
Copper-nickel alloys
Nickel-copper alloys
Silver solder
Nickel (passive)
Chromium-iron (passive)
Silver
Graphite
Gold
Platinum
PROTECTED END (*cathodic, or most noble*)

* The metals and alloys bracketed are considered
the best to use together in marine application.

498. Why is the galvanic series of metals important to a boat owner? Because a knowledge of the position of metals in the series will enable him to select metals for a given purpose which will be compatible.

499. What are the principal hazards against which a boatman must guard? There are a good many "hazards of the sea," as the insurance companies call them. In a power or auxiliary boat the worst hazard is explosion. Fire is a close second. Sinking is rather rare but capsizing in small sailboats is not at all unusual. Running aground can be serious if it happens on a rock, but on sand or mud it is more annoying than risky.

When running in a fog there is a risk of collision, and steamer lanes should be avoided under such conditions. Navigating in fog when close to shore also increases the possibility of running aground. And there is always a possibility of falling overboard.

500. What is the Yacht Safety Bureau?   This organization tests equipment submitted to them by marine manufacturers. If the product meets certain standards it is given a YSB listing.

501. What must you do if you are in a boating accident?   The Federal Boating Act requires that you stop, offer assistance, identify yourself, and, if the accident is serious, make a written report.

502. Who must file reports of boating accidents?   A written report of an accident must be filed by a boat operator if (1) there was loss of life; (2) injury incapacitated any individual for more than 72 hours; (3) physical damage to property was in excess of $100.

503. Where should accident reports be sent?   Accident reports should be made to the Coast Guard or the state agency that numbered the boat. Some states require reports even if one has already been made to the Coast Guard.

504. How do the Coast Guard and the marine insurance companies classify fires?   There are three recognized types of fires. Combustion of materials such as wood, upholstery, fabrics, etc., is a Class A fire. Class B fires are those caused by liquids or gases, while Class C fires originate in electric systems—overheated wires, short circuits, etc.

505. What is the proper way to fight a fire?   First, of course, it should be determined what kind of fire it is—Class A, B, or C—and where its base is located. If possible, seal off the fire by closing all air vents to shut off its oxygen supply—no oxygen, no fire. Turn off all fuel lines to engine and stove. Throw battery switches to the off position, no matter what type fire it may be.

Direct a fire extinguisher at the base of the fire as quickly as possible to prevent its spreading. A bucket of water may put out a small Class A fire, but one of the approved extinguishers must be used on Classes B and C. The latter may turn into Class A if it gets headway enough to ignite woodwork or other surrounding materials.

For boats with enclosed engine compartments an automatic fire extinguisher system is recommended. This is set off by the temperature rise caused by a fire.

506. How do you fight a Class A fire? Usually water will extinguish such a blaze. Soda-acid or foam fire extinguishers also are recommended for Class A fires.

Blazing objects can also be thrown overboard in an emergency. Try not to let the fire gain headway. Act fast.

507. What is the best way to fight a Class B fire? Don't use water on this type fire; water only causes it to spread. Carbon dioxide (CO_2), foam, or dry chemical extinguishers are best for this kind of blaze. Many boats are equipped with built-in CO_2 systems that are automatic.

There is one exception to the foregoing; that is blazing alcohol. This can be extinguished with water, but care must be taken not to spread the fire.

508. How do you locate a Class C fire? Unlike Class A and B fires, Class C fires don't usually start with a blaze, but may smoulder for some time before igniting. Such fires can, and frequently do, start in hidden spaces such as behind bulkheads or upholstery, and the first warning may be the smell. If you smell smoke, but can't locate the source, pull the main switch at once, shut off all fuel lines to engine and stove.

It may be necessary to rip up upholstery or to tear out joiner work to get at the source.

If not attended to promptly, a Class C fire will probably become a Class A fire; that is, it will ignite the surrounding materials.

Once the current is shut off the area can safely be drenched with water to quench any incipient blaze.

509. What is the usual cause of a Class C fire?   Faulty electric wiring is most often found to be the cause. Such fires can occur when no one is aboard the boat unless all current has been shut off at a main switch.

Every boat equipped with electricity should have a main switch (or several switches) which will cut off all current. And such switches should always be pulled before the boat is left.

510. How does one cope with a Class C fire?   Under no circumstances use water or a liquid extinguisher on this type of fire, particularly if high voltage current is involved. There would be real danger of being electrocuted if a liquid extinguisher were used.

The proper extinguisher for Class C fires is either dry chemical or carbon dioxide (CO_2).

511. What can be done to prevent fire on a boat?   Care is the answer. Be careful with cigarettes and matches. Be constantly on the alert for leaks of gasoline or stove fuel, if liquid or gas. Don't smoke in your berth and prohibit guests from doing so.

Take care when cooking not to allow grease to ignite and flare up. Be extra careful when pouring fuel into a stove. Burners should not be lighted during fueling.

Fire can be caused by faulty electric wiring. Don't take chances; have all wiring installed by a qualified technician. If 110-volt current is used when alongside a dock, be particularly careful of short circuits and sparks.

512. What three types of fire extinguishers are approved by the National Fire Protection Association for use on boats?   Carbon dioxide (CO_2) and dry chemical for class B and C fires. Foam for Class A and B fires.

513. Why are carbon tetrachloride extinguishers no longer approved by safety authorities for marine use?   When this liquid strikes a fire it turns into a highly toxic gas which, when breathed into the lungs, can have extremely harmful effects.

514. What are the principal causes of explosion aboard a boat?   Gasoline vapor or escaping cooking gas are the most frequent causes of explosions on boats. Both are heavier than air, so they tend to accumulate in the bilges and along the cabin floors, where the slightest spark will set them off.

515. When is a gasoline explosion most likely to occur? The danger of a gasoline vapor explosion is greatest when (or just after) fuel tanks are filled. As the liquid enters the tank it expels the vapor inside; this vapor is heavier than air, so it seeks the lowest point it can find. Being highly explosive, the slightest spark will set it off.

The same hazard exists if there is a fuel leak from a carburetor or fuel line. Liquid gasoline will burn but won't explode; the vapor is the more dangerous element.

516. What precautions should be observed against explosion? Precautions fall into two categories: First, details of the boat's construction and the arrangement of her fuel, ventilation, and fire-fighting systems. Standards for such installations have been set by the Yacht Safety Bureau. Second, personal care by all aboard to make sure that no exposed flame or spark occurs while gasoline is being taken on; also, that no fuel is spilled into the bilge or other spaces aboard.

517. What causes cooking gas leaks? Carelessness is the primary cause of leaks, either carelessness in making the necessary pipe connections between the tank and the stove or carelessness in shutting off the gas after the stove is used. There is a risk that a burner may be turned on inadvertently, thus causing gas to escape. There are several ways this can happen if great care is not observed in handling such a stove. Also, a lighted burner may be blown out without the cook noticing it.

518. What is the safest stove for a boat? The old-fashioned coal stove is the safest. It can burn coal, charcoal, wood, or briquettes. But no stove is perfectly safe on a boat. Where fire exists there is danger. Also, from a coal stove there is danger of suffocation if a cabin is closed tight while the stove is burning. Or a backdraft down the stove pipe can force the deadly fumes of combustion into the cabin. Adequate ventilation is always absolutely necessary in a confined space, such as a boat's cabin.

519. What is the best source of information on prevention of fire and explosion on boats? The National Fire Protection Association, 60 Batterymarch Street, Boston 10, Massachusetts, publishes a book (NFPA No. 302—50¢) called *Fire Protection Standards for Motor Craft.* It cannot be too strongly recommended that every owner of a power-driven boat read this book and follow its recommendations.

520. What should be done if a boat is sinking? Obviously, the first thing to do is to try to stop water from entering the hull. It would be wise also for all hands to don life jackets. If a dinghy or life raft is carried on deck, it should be launched, just to be on the safe side.

Distress signals can be made, to call for help, if the leak is beyond control.

521. What can be done to stop small leaks while afloat? Usually, the best that can be done is to stuff caulking cotton in a leaky seam from inside. This is only a temporary measure, however. The boat should be hauled out at the first opportunity and the leaky seam permanently recaulked.

In the absence of caulking cotton, any cloth can be used.

522. What can be done to stop large leaks when afloat? Such a leak is most likely to be caused by striking a piece of wreckage or a rock which may fracture a fiber-glass hull or a plank in a wooden hull. Sometimes the fracture can be closed from inside by covering it with canvas or even a blanket, backed up with suitable shoring to hold the cloth against the water pressure.

In the case of a wooden boat, a sheet of lead can be nailed over the cloth patch.

If the leak can't be stopped from inside, it will be necessary to get a piece of canvas over it from outside.

523. If it is impossible to stop a leak, what is the best course of action? Head for the nearest shoal water as fast as possible and beach her before she sinks. In case the boat is without power to maneuver, the last resort is to abandon ship. Make every effort to call for help and see that all hands have on life jackets. Save valuables.

If the boat will sink in deep water attach some floating object to

her with a long line so it will act as a buoy by which the wreck can
later be located.

524. What should be done if someone falls overboard? First,
heave over a life preserver, which should always be kept handy. Even
a buoyant cushion of the Coast Guard–approved variety will do for
a small boat. Then get back to the swimmer as soon as possible.

As a sailboat will jibe quicker than it will come about, it is best to
jibe over and come up to windward of the swimmer. This allows the
boat to make a lee and also to drift down slowly toward the man overboard. Heave a line to him as soon as he comes within range. Get over
some sort of boarding ladder if possible.

A powerboat should follow the same procedure. In addition, if
there is danger of the victim being fouled in the propeller, the clutch
should be slipped until he is well clear. Then the boat should be put
into a tight turn at high speed to get up to windward of the swimmer
as quickly as possible.

525. Is lightning a hazard on a boat? Yes, but not a very serious
one. Lightning occasionally strikes the masthead of the tallest mast
and runs down the wire rigging. It can do damage to the boat but seldom to those aboard. However, it is well, if caught in a thunder and
lightning squall, not to touch any of the wire rigging.

**526. What measures should be taken to protect a boat against light-
ning?** The principal precaution to take against lightning is to make
sure the wire rigging is grounded, in other words, that it is making
contact with the water. On some sailboats the chain plates to which
the rigging is secured are permanently connected to a keel bolt. A
simple form of temporary protection is to make contact with the
water by hanging overboard a piece of chain that is shackled to a
stay.

**527. If, when abandoning ship, there is no dinghy and the crew
must take to the water, what precautions should be taken?** All
should put on life jackets. Unless there is the prospect of being picked
up at once by a rescuing vessel, all hands should be lashed together
loosely so as not to get separated. This is particularly important in
rough water or at night.

528. In northern latitudes what is the greatest danger to being adrift for a long period in a life raft?   Cold weather is a considerable danger, as is the possibility of being run down by an unseeing vessel in fog.

529. In southern latitudes what is the principal hazard to being adrift for long periods in a life raft?   Exposure to sun will be the greatest hazard in most instances. If you should ever have occasion to abandon ship, be sure to include some means of protection from the sun.

530. What frequency is the international radiophone distress channel?   The frequency is 2182 kilocycles.

531. What authority is responsible for the registration and numbering of pleasure craft?   Under the 1958 Federal Boating Act, any state may take over the registration and numbering of pleasure craft by enactment of a suitable state law and a numbering system approved by the U.S. Coast Guard. All numbering must conform to the uniform national system, and states must agree to extend reciprocity for at least ninety days to boats from another state with an approved system.

Most states have adopted a federally approved system, but where they have not, the Coast Guard has continued to exercise its traditional numbering function.

532. What boats must be numbered?   The Federal Boating Act of 1958 states that all undocumented vessels propelled by machinery of more than 10 horsepower must be numbered. This includes inboards, outboards, and auxiliaries, regardless of size.

533. Must a number be renewed?   Yes. If a number is not renewed by the date of its expiration, it will become invalid at that time.

534. Can a boat registration be transferred?   No. If a boat is sold, the new owner must make an application for a number.

535. How must a number be displayed.   The number awarded must be painted or attached to each side of the bow so as to be distinctly visible and clearly legible. The letters and numbers must be of plain block design, not less than three inches in height, and of a color that will contrast with the background.

536. Where may more information on individual state laws be obtained? The Outboard Boating Club of America (307 North Michigan Avenue, Chicago 1, Illinois) has published an excellent series covering states and federal boating laws in detail. This is complete with equipment requirements, trailer laws, etc.

537. What boats are entitled to documentation? Under navigation laws administered by the Bureau of Customs, a vessel of not less than five net tons, owned by a United States citizen, and used exclusively for pleasure may be documented as a yacht.

538. What are the advantages of having a yacht documented? A documented yacht is exempt from numbering in all states. She can be taken into any state without having to obtain a state license. Documentation also makes cruising between the United States and foreign countries easier, as it is not necessary to clear U.S. Customs before leaving the country, and a yacht of fifteen gross tons or less is not required to reenter the United States through customs. Documentation makes financing the purchase of a yacht easier and facilitates the transfer of title to such vessels. Documented yachts have the privilege of flying the United States yacht ensign in foreign waters. This is a doubtful advantage, however, since most American yachts, regardless of size or documentation, fly the yacht ensign at home and abroad.

539. How much does it cost to have a yacht documented? At present, it costs nothing. However, there has been legislation pending to establish a one-time fee of eight dollars.

540. Who enforces boating laws? The U.S. Coast Guard has law enforcement authority on all navigable waters of the United States. Even in states that administer their own boating laws, the Coast Guard continues to patrol federal waterways.

541. How does the U.S. Coast Guard carry out law enforcement? If hailed for a boarding inspection while under way, a yacht must come to a stop and maneuver to permit the boarding officer to come aboard. There is a $100 fine for failure to submit to boarding while under way. If at anchor or tied to a dock, however, you are not required to submit to a boarding inspection. The boarding officer then may not come aboard without your permission.

542. What is the United States Coast Guard Auxiliary? The USCGA was authorized by Congress in 1939 as a nonmilitary, voluntary organization of boat owners and others interested in boats, the water, and safety. Members have no law enforcement authority, but through example, advice, instruction, and their annual courtesy examination program, they assist the Coast Guard by encouraging compliance with rules and regulations.

543. Does the Coast Guard have the authority to impose fines? Yes. They may level fines for failure to obey rules of the road and other regulations. Among the latter are laws that require boats to be operated in a safe and courteous manner.

544. In terms of the law, what is meant by "motorboat"? A motorboat is any vessel up to 65 feet overall which is propelled by machinery. Excluded are steam tugs and towboats, but included are auxiliary sailing vessels of all types.

545. As defined by law, what are the four classes of motorboats?
Class A—any motorboat less than 16 feet overall.
Class 1—16 feet or over and less than 26 feet.
Class 2—26 feet or over and less than 40 feet.
Class 3—40 feet or over and less than 65 feet.

546. What is Coast Guard–approved equipment? Approved equipment is assigned a number which is listed in a Coast Guard booklet (CG–190). Approved types of equipment required on motorboats include lifesaving devices, fire extinguishers, and carburetor backfire flame arrestors. If you cruise navigable waters, your equipment should be Coast Guard–approved.

547. How can one tell if an item of equipment is Coast Guard–approved? Approval numbers and the classes of boats for which the item meets federal regulations (if applicable) should be prominently and permanently displayed on the item's label.

548. What lifesaving devices are required by law to be aboard motorboats? All motorboat classes require some kind of approved lifesaving equipment for each person aboard. Classes A, 1, and 2 vessels may use an approved buoyant cushion or a buoyant vest, in place of the standard life preservers of jacket design. Class 3 vessels require approved jacket-type life preservers or approved ring buoys.

549. According to the Coast Guard definition, what is the difference between a life preserver and a buoyant vest? A life preserver provides about 22 pounds of buoyancy while a buoyant vest gives about 16. Either may be designed to be worn like a collar, but only life preservers are made to be worn like a jacket.

550. What fire extinguishers are required by law for motorboats? The only type of boat exempt from requirements covering fire extinguishers is open outboards. All inboard motorboats and outboards not of open construction of Class A and Class 1 must have at least one approved hand-portable type fire extinguisher aboard. Boats in Classes 2 and 3 may be required to have at least two or more portable extinguishers of specified types. All fire extinguishers must be in good working order.

551. Are motorboats required to carry horns? A horn or whistle, hand- mouth- or power-operated, capable of producing a blast of at least two seconds duration is required on all Class 1 and 2 motorboats. It must be audible for at least one-half mile on Class 1 boats and at least one mile on Class 2 vessels. A power-operated horn is mandatory on Class 3 vessels. Class A vessels are not required to carry a horn, but they must comply with the proper sound signals as specified in the Rules of the Road.

552. Are any vessels required to carry bells? A bell is required on Class 2 and 3 vessels. It should be one "which, when struck, produces a clear bell-like tone of full, round characteristics." Some states also require smaller vessels to have bells.

Bells are used when vessels are at anchor in a fog to warn of their position. Consult Coast Guard regulations for proper use.

IX. MARINE ENGINES

Introduction. Marine engines for pleasure boats fall into two classes, internal expansion and internal combustion. The reciprocating internal expansion engine operates by steam. The steam is made from fresh water which is heated in a boiler, usually by oil or coal. In the early years of this century yacht's launches were powered by small steam engines with naphtha-fired boilers and they were called naphtha launches. There is a revival in the use of small steam engines for pleasure boats, and suitable coal- or oil-fired power plants are again being made.

The second class—the internal combustion engine—is again divided into two types, gasoline and diesel. The former depends on the explosion of a charge of mixed air and gasoline being set off by an electric spark, while the explosion in the diesel engine is induced by ultra high compression in the cylinders, no spark being needed. These engines operate on the principal that when a gas (in this case a mixture of diesel oil and air) is sufficiently compressed it becomes heated to the point of incandescence. This causes it to explode, which develops the necessary power to push down the pistons in the cylinders of a diesel engine.

Other types of engines are in various stages of development—for example, the so-called gas turbine, which is not a reciprocating engine at all. Gas turbines are purely rotary engines whose power is developed by a highly compressed gas impinging on a series of vanes which are attached to the periphery of a rotor that is integral with the main drive shaft. Several engines of this type are in limited use, mostly by the armed forces or by government agencies. It looks as though their civilian use is a long way off.

553. How many types of internal combustion engines are there?

Internal combustion engines are divided into various types such as inboard and outboard; two-cycle and four-cycle (also called two-stroke and four-stroke); gasoline and diesel. Kerosene is also used in certain heavy-duty engines, mostly by fishermen. They operate on the same principle as gasoline engines.

554. How many systems compose an internal combustion engine?
Internal combustion engines combine six systems; fuel, ignition,
lubrication, cooling, exhaust, and drive. Developing useful power
from such engines also requires controls and drive (propeller) shafts.
The latter are usually equipped with gears for reversing their direction and frequently with reduction gears to change the speed ratio between engine and propeller. For example, with 2:1 reduction gears an
engine shaft rotating at 2,000 r.p.m. would turn a propeller at 1,000
r.p.m.

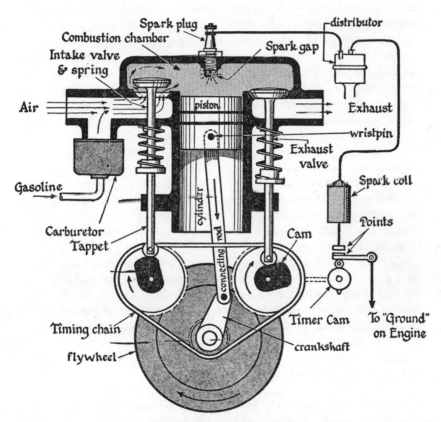

Parts of an internal combustion gasoline engine (schematic drawing)

**555. What is meant by the term "over-square" when applied to an
internal combustion engine?** This means that the internal diameter,

or bore, of its cylinders exceeds the travel or stroke of its pistons. For example; an engine with a bore of 3¼ inches and a stroke of 3 inches is over-square. Contrariwise, if bore and stroke are equal the engine is said to be square. If the stroke exceeds the bore the engine is under-square.

556. What does two-cycle mean? This term describes an internal combustion engine that receives a power impulse in each of its cylinders every second stroke. If works this way: The spark plug ignites the fuel in the combustion chamber which causes the piston to travel toward the crank shaft. As the piston travels it also compresses the explosive mixture of air and gasoline in the engine's base.

When the piston is at the end of its power stroke it uncovers two openings in the cylinder walls, called ports. One of these is the exhaust port and the burned gases escape through it. The other is the intake port, and through this the compressed gas in the engine's base enters the cylinder's combustion chamber by means of a bypass channel between the base and the combustion chamber.

The piston now reverses its direction, moving up in the cylinder. This further compresses the gas in the combustion chamber while at the same time a new charge of fuel and air is sucked into the base.

When the piston reaches its topmost position the spark plug ignites the compressed gas; the piston plunges downward on its power stroke. The piston receives a power impulse every time it reaches its topmost position.

Such a cycle makes it possible to develop maximum horsepower for a given number of cylinders, but it is wasteful of fuel and lubricating oil, which is mixed with the fuel to lubricate the piston, the connecting rod, and crank shaft bearings. The presence of the oil in the gas mixture tends to form carbon deposits on spark plugs, which should be cleaned frequently to assure satisfactory performance.

Engines which operate on this principle are also called two-stroke.

Most outboards are two-cycle engines.

557. What does four-cycle mean? This term describes the operation of a type of reciprocating internal combustion engine in which the power stroke occurs every fourth travel of the piston. The four strokes of the piston are intake (down), compression (up), explosion (down), exhaust (up).

On the intake stroke the cam shaft raises the intake valve, the down stroke of the piston sucks a mixture of fuel and air from the carburetor, through the intake manifold, into the cylinder.

On the compression stroke the intake valve is closed by the cam shaft, and the fuel mixture is compressed.

When the piston reaches the top of its travel, and the mixture is at its maximum compression, the spark plug ignites the mixture, which explodes and forces the piston down in the power stroke.

When the piston reaches its lowest position the exhaust valve is opened by the cam shaft; the piston is pushed up by the crank shaft; the exhaust (used) gases are expelled from the cylinder. At the top of this stroke the exhaust valve closes and the intake valve opens. The cycle repeats on the next down stroke.

558. What is the difference between reciprocating and rotary motion in a marine engine? Reciprocating motion is the up-and-down movement of a piston within a cylinder. Rotary motion is the turning of a shaft such as a drive or cam shaft.

559. How does a diesel engine work? When air is compressed it is also heated. If compressed enough it gets so hot that when fuel is injected it will cause combustion. This is the principle on which diesel engines operate. Air is forced into a cylinder on a down stroke of the piston by a blower. The up stroke compresses it to a point where it is incandescent. When the piston reaches its topmost position, fuel oil is injected under very high pressure through a cam-operated fuel injector. The oil ignites, thus developing the power that forces the piston down on its power stroke. When the piston reaches its lowest point it uncovers ports in the cylinder walls through which fresh air is introduced into the cylinder by a blower. At this point the exhaust valve in the cylinder head opens—actuated by a cam—and the burned gas is expelled, or scavenged, by the fresh air under pressure. The exhaust valve closes. Then the piston moves up, closing the air ports and compressing the air in the cylinder. Thus the cycle is completed.

In the case of a multicylinder engine the events described are taking place in each cylinder, but at different times.

This is a brief description of the operation of a two-cycle diesel engine.

A four-cycle diesel engine operates on the same principle as the two-cycle engine; that is, the explosion of the fuel charge is caused by high compression, not by a spark as in a gasoline engine. But the power impulse occurs half as often as in a two-cycle engine.

560. What is the function of injectors on a diesel engine?   The units through which fuel is forced into a diesel's cylinders against the elevated pressure which exists at the moment of ignition is called an injector. There is one for each cylinder.

561. What is the function of the blower on a diesel engine?   The blower supplies the continuous flow of fresh air under pressure needed by a diesel engine both for combustion and scavenging, or exhaust.

562. What are synchronous motors?   A twin-screw boat, having two engines rotating in opposite directions, should have them synchronized so they operate at identical speeds.

563. What is meant by the term "compression" in an internal combustion engine?   This is what takes place in the upper part of a cylinder (the combustion chamber) when the piston moves up after having sucked a charge of fuel mixture into the cylinder on its previous down, or suction, stroke. The piston's upward movement compresses the charge, ready for firing by the spark.

564. What are the advantages of an outboard engine over an inboard?   Maintenance is easier on an outboard because it can be easily removed from the boat. Outboards are also easier to service because they do not have a separate oil system. Oil is mixed right in with the gasoline in a mixture stipulated by the manufacturer.

565. If an outboard engine falls overboard, what should be done?   If the engine can be recovered immediately, it can probably be reconditioned. Until it can be properly dried and overhauled, it should be kept immersed in fresh water. Slow drying causes interior parts to rust.

566. What is meant by an inboard/outboard (outdrive) engine?   This is a recent development which combines the advantages of both the inboard and the outboard engine. The power unit (engine) is permanently installed within the boat, away aft. The drive unit, which can be tipped up and turned from side to side like an outboard engine, is bolted to the boat's transom and is connected directly to the power unit.

Such installations may consist of a power unit from one maker and a drive unit from another. However, there are some manufacturers who supply a complete package of both the power and drive units.

567. What maintenance is particularly required on inboard/outboard engines? The lower drive unit must be constantly checked to make sure that the gears are well greased. Water seepage that goes unnoticed can cause considerable damage.

568. What is an engine's ignition system? This is the electric system whose function is to ignite the fuel in an engine's cylinder. It commences at the generator or the battery and terminates at the spark plugs and includes the distributor, the coil, the condenser, and the wiring.

569. What is the purpose of a generator? Batteries, which supply electric current aboard a boat, run down as current is consumed. This current has to be replaced, and that is the function of a generator—it makes electricity and feeds it to the batteries. Modern marine engines are equipped with a generator to keep the starter battery charged, but on boats with much electric equipment such as telephone, radio direction finders, etc., it is necessary to have a second generator and more batteries.

570. What is a magneto? It is a form of electric generator used on outboard motors. It takes the place of the battery–spark coil combination of inboard engines. It generates the high tension electricity required by spark plugs.

571. What function does an alternator perform? This is an electrical device of relatively recent development which takes the place of the older and less efficient generator. An alternator generates alternating current (AC) which is converted to direct current (DC) by a rectifier or silicon diode. Because the alternator can be run at several times engine speed without damage, it is capable of delivering current to keep batteries charged even when the engine which drives it is turning over slowly.

Alternators have several advantages over generators: They are more reliable, easier to maintain, and do not tend to spark to the same degree.

572. What advantage has an alternator over a DC generator? It will keep a battery charged up even when the engine is turning over slowly. It is small for its capacity, and it eliminates dangerous sparking.

573. Does an alternator generate direct current, as a generator does? No. It generates alternating current.

574. How does the alternating current from an alternator get converted to direct current which is required for charging batteries. It is passed through a rectifier which converts it to direct current.

575. What is a silicon diode? This is another name for the current rectifier of an alternator. As an alternator generates alternating current and a battery can be charged only with direct current, it is obvious that a device that will convert AC to DC is required. This is the function of a silicon diode, which can be likened to a check valve that permits a current flow in only one direction—in this case, direct current.

576. What is the purpose of a distributor? As the name implies, a distributor's job is to distribute the charge of high-tension electricity, which originates as a low-tension charge (6 or 12 volts) at the battery or the generator and is converted to high tension current (10,000 volts) by an induction coil. The function of the distributor is to direct high-tension current to the spark plugs at the precise instant when the piston has compressed the explosive fuel mixture in the cylinder and the connecting rod bearing on the crankshaft has just passed top dead center.

When the high-tension current reaches the spark plug it jumps across the spark gap (a distance about equal to the thickness of a dime) igniting the fuel and causing an explosion which drives the piston down, thus delivering power to the crankshaft.

577. What is a timer? See distributor.

578. In a marine engine, what is the meaning of timing? If an engine is to operate efficiently it is vitally important that its timing be correct. The term includes both mechanical and electrical timing.

Mechanical timing embraces the cam shaft, timing gears, etc., which determine the instant at which the intake and exhaust valves open and close.

Electrical timing also involves the gears that operate the distributor.

579. What is the function of the breaker points on a gasoline engine? Breaker points are an important part of a distributor and serve to interrupt the high-tension current flowing from the secondary winding of the induction coil to the spark plugs. The proper adjustment of the breaker point gap is critical if an engine is to run properly. This gap, which is tested by a feeler gauge, is usually about .018 inch to .020 inch. Breaker points get pitted from the passage of high-tension current and must be filed smooth or replaced occasionally. This should be done only by a competent mechanic.

580. What is a condenser? This is an extremely important component of an ignition system. It serves, along with the coil, to greatly increase the voltage of the current flowing to the spark plugs. In other words, it helps to convert low-tension current (12 volts) to high-tension current (25,000 volts).

581. What is the function of a condenser? This is an electrical device that is part of a distributor. Its function is to prevent high-voltage current discharge across the breaker points of the distributor when the primary circuit is interrupted or broken.

582. What is the function of a circuit breaker? This is the unit of a generator regulator that allows current to pass from the generator to the battery, but which opens automatically when the generator is not charging, thus preventing the battery from discharging back into the generator. It is, in fact, an automatic switch.

583. What is an induction coil? Usually referred to simply as a coil, this unit is an important part of the electrical system of all internal combustion engines using spark plugs (excepting those equipped with high-tension magnetos). Actually, an induction coil is a small transformer consisting of two windings of fine wire—primary and secondary—on a core of soft iron wires, laid parallel.

The primary (inner) winding receives low-tension current from the battery, generator, or magneto. The sudden interruption of the flow of current to the primary winding causes a discharge of magnetic waves into the secondary (high-tension) winding, which induces a high-tension current to develop. This current is transmitted to the spark plugs.

584. What is the function of a commutator?   This is the device—cylindrical in form—on the end of the shaft of a motor or generator which distributes the current to (motor) or from (generator) the instrument's coils. It is divided into segments, insulated from each other, against which carbon brushes make contact and transmit the current as required.

585. What form does an extra generator usually take?   There are two kinds of extra generators for use aboard a boat. The simplest is belt-driven by the main propulsion engine and, of course, only generates when that engine is running.

Where there is much current-consuming equipment on a yacht, such as refrigerators, electric stoves, deep-freezers, etc., it is necessary to have a separate power plant to run a generator that can be operated almost continuously to keep up the batteries. Some self-contained generators are equipped with automatic self-starters, which cause the charging engine to start whenever an increase in the electric demand requires extra current.

586. What is a spark plug?   This is a unit made up of several parts that delivers a high-tension electric spark to the fuel charge in a cylinder's combustion chamber at precisely the instant required. A heavily insulated wire carries the electricity to the plug's electrode, which is insulated from the body of the plug with porcelain. The body's lower rim has a metal projection which almost touches the end of the electrode. The space between the two is the spark gap; it is about equal to the thickness of a dime and varies somewhat, according to the make of engine. Across this gap a high-tension spark leads to ignite the fuel.

587. What functions do batteries perform on boats? Batteries can be regarded as reservoirs in which direct current electricity is stored. In fact they are called storage batteries. Batteries supply the power required to start a boat's engine, the current to provide lights and to operate all the electronic equipment aboard.

Batteries run down as current is drawn from them, and they must be constantly recharged to be kept in good condition. This is the function of a generator.

588. What are the principal parts of a storage battery? The case in which all the parts are contained is usually hard rubber but may be made of glass, an acid-resistant alloy, or certain plastics. There are positive and negative plates within each cell, each separated by a suitable insulator. The negative plates are connected to a negative terminal, or post, on top of the battery, and the positive plates are also connected to their own terminal. Each cell has a ventilated plug so that the battery can be tested for its charge state and distilled water can be added as required. A solution consisting of water and sulfuric acid, called electrolyte, is necessary to activate the battery. Without this solution there would be no chemical action in the battery, and it is this action that generates electricity.

589. In what voltages are storage batteries available? Each cell in a storage battery supplies 2 volts so that a 6-volt battery will have 3 cells, a 12-volt battery has 6 cells, and a 24-volt battery will have 12 cells. Most boat batteries are either 6- or 12-volt.

590. What kinds of batteries are there? Two. (1) Primary or dry cells. These are expendable and are discarded when they run down. (2) Storage batteries that can be recharged many times. The latter is the type used in the ignition system and for other purposes aboard a boat. The dry cell is used mostly in flashlights, radios, etc.

591. What does a convertor do? This is an electrical device that converts the direct current (DC) supplied by a storage battery into alternating current (AC) which is needed to operate many of the conveniences found aboard modern cruising boats.

592. How does an engine's starter work?   This is a sort of chain reaction. Pressing the starter button sends current to a solenoid, which is in fact a heavy-duty, electrically operated switch. The solenoid in turn sends current through a heavy cable from the battery to the starting motor which, by means of its Bendix drive, turns over the engine's flywheel, thus setting in motion the cycle of operations that causes the engine to run.

593. What is the purpose of a Bendix drive?   This is an ingenious device used to start internal combustion engines. Its principal element is a special pinion gear wheel which slides back and forth on its drive shaft. When the starter switch button is pushed, the Bendix pinion gear slides out on its shaft and its teeth engage matching teeth cut around the periphery of the engine's flywheel. A powerful motor turns the Bendix gear which causes the flywheel of the engine to rotate. The latter is integral with the engine's crankshaft, so it can be seen the Bendix drive provides the impulse necessary to start the engine.

As soon as the engine starts, the Bendix gear slides back on its shaft, thus disengaging its teeth from those of the flywheel. When the person starting the engine ceases pressing the starter button the Bendix motor stops.

594. What is the function of a carburetor?   This is the instrument that supplies gasoline and air in correct proportions to an internal combustion engine.

595. How does a carburetor work?   The down strokes of the pistons in an internal combustion engine (the intake, not the power strokes) cause a partial vacuum which is transmitted, via the intake manifold, to the carburetor, causing a rush of fresh air through its mixing chamber.

In the mixing chamber there is a small nozzle through which gasoline is introduced in minute quantities into the passing air stream which vaporizes it. This vapor rushes through the intake manifold, past the intake poppet valves, into the combustion chambers of the cylinders, where it is compressed and exploded.

To provide a constant supply of gasoline to its jet (or jets) a carburetor has a small reservoir called a float chamber in which a constant fuel level is maintained by a small float which meters the amount of fuel entering the chamber.

Modern carburetors usually have two jets: a low-speed, or idling, jet and a high-speed jet. As their names imply these jets only function under appropriate conditions. The orifices in the jets of some carburetors can be adjusted by means of needle valves, in others they are fixed. As the size of the orifice is a critical and very sensitive factor in an engine's operation, adjustments should be made only by qualified persons.

A carburetor also has two butterfly valves: one in its intake, controlling the air flow, called the choke valve; one in its throat, which meters the amount of mixture (gasoline and air) that flows to the cylinders and thus determines the engine's speed. This valve is called the throttle.

Several manufacturers make marine carburetors, and each to his own design, yet all of them work on the same principle, differing only in details.

596. What is a throttle?   This is a device, usually a butterfly valve, in a carburetor by which the amount of fuel entering the cylinders— and hence the speed of the engine—can be controlled. It is one of the most important controls on an engine, and the lever that operates it should be conveniently situated so the helmsman can change speed at will.

597. What does a manifold do?   On an engine of more than one cylinder it is necessary to distribute the ingoing fuel mixture from the carburetor to each cylinder in exactly even amounts, and this is done through a unit containing carefully designed passages called an intake manifold.

Also, exhaust gases have to be carried away from each cylinder, which is the function of an exhaust manifold.

598. Why does a modern engine have a fuel pump?   Gravity feed, which was standard practice years ago for fuel systems, is, for safety's sake, no longer approved. For this reason it is necessary to pump the fuel from the tank to the carburetor, so a fuel pump has become standard equipment on engines.

599. What is the purpose of a backfire trap or flame arrestor?   This is a fitting attached to the air intake of a carburetor to prevent flames from emitting should the engine backfire. It is a safety device that is a part of all modern engines and is Coast Guard–required. Its principal element is a fine-mesh metal screen which admits air to the carburetor but prevents flames from passing in the opposite direction. This screen should be kept clean if the engine is to operate satisfactorily.

600. What is meant by the term "vapor lock"?   If a fuel line from the tank to the fuel pump gets overheated for any reason, it may cause the liquid fuel within it to vaporize causing the engine to slow down or stall.

601. How can vapor lock be temporarily overcome?   The temporary cure is to let the fuel line cool off. This can be accomplished by wrapping it with wet cloths or by simply waiting until the engine cools off and then running it slow enough so it won't overheat.

602. What measures can be taken to prevent vapor lock?   The usual cure is to reroute the fuel line to avoid hot areas or to insulate it, or both. If vapor lock persists, an electric fuel pump can be installed at the gasoline tank to push the fuel along.

603. Why is it necessary to cool an internal combustion engine?   All internal combustion engines develop heat from friction of their moving parts and from the combustion of fuel in their cylinders. If such an engine was not cooled it would soon get red hot and cease operation. Overheating can cause major damage to an engine.

604. How many types of cooling systems are there for internal combustion engines?   Three systems of cooling are used: air cooling; open-system water cooling; and closed-system water cooling.

605. How does an air cooling system work?   This system depends on a free flow of cool air around the engine which has fins cast on its outer surface to dissipate the heat it develops. Such an engine can be installed only in an open boat and is of low horsepower.

606. How does an open water cooling system function? In this type of system water—be it salt or fresh—is sucked in through a strainer from outside the boat by a water pump. This pump then forces the water to circulate through the engine's water jacket, cooling the cylinders, valves, and other moving parts as well as lubricating oil. Finally the water is injected into the exhaust line near the point where it leaves the engine. This turns the water to steam which, in turn, cools the exhaust gas, the exhaust line, and the muffler. Finally, the used steam and gas mixture emerges from the exhaust pipe overboard.

607. What is the difference between an open and a closed water cooling system? In a closed system no water is taken from outside the boat. The cooling water is fresh, never salt, and is recirculated around the engine's cooling system by a pump, as in the open system. Instead of being dissipated with the exhaust gases, however, the water is cooled by passing through a heat exchanger before being recirculated by the water pump.

608. What is the advantage of a closed (fresh water) cooling system? For boats that operate in salt water the principal advantage is that no salt is introduced into the circulating system. Salt causes the formation of scale inside water jackets which will eventually reduce their efficiency. It also induces rust to form more rapidly than does fresh water.

The foregoing comments do not apply to boats that operate in fresh water, of course. But there is another advantage to a closed cooling system: The temperature of the circulating water in an engine is important to its efficiency. If it runs too cool the engine won't heat up to its most efficient operating temperature. In an open system a thermostat is supposed to maintain the correct temperature, but doesn't always do so. It is easier to control water temperature in a closed system, so the engine runs better and lasts longer.

609. What is a heat exchanger? This is a device for cooling the circulating water in a closed or fresh water cooling system. It takes in cold water from outside the vessel and circulates it around pipes in which fresh cooling water is carried. This cools the fresh water to the temperature suitable for the best operation of the engine.

610. How can one tell if an engine is overheating? Practically all modern marine engines are equipped with a gauge that shows the temperature of the cooling water. By consulting this gauge, which should be done frequently, it is possible to keep track of cooling water temperature.

611. What is the purpose of a thermostat? This automatic device is installed in the cooling water system to control the water temperature. If the engine runs too hot or too cold, look to the thermostat. It may be out of order or need replacing.

612. What happens if an engine runs too hot? Since metal expands when heated it is vitally important that an engine not be allowed to overheat. If it does so to excess, it should be stopped at once and the cause of overheating be determined and corrected at once, or before the engine is restarted.

613. What happens if an engine runs too cold? It loses efficiency because there is not enough heat to properly vaporize the fuel. Also, since metal expands slightly when heated, some of the more sensitive clearances between operating parts, such as pistons and cylinder walls, may not attain their optimum conditions.

614. What causes an engine to overheat? Overheating is usually caused by an interruption of the cooling water supply. In an outboard motor or a two-cycle engine overheating can be caused by insufficient lubricating oil in the gasoline. Overheating of a four-cycle engine can also be caused by insufficient lubricating oil reaching the moving parts, causing excessive friction. A possible third cause of overheating is running with the spark retarded, but this is unusual.

615. What should be done if an engine overheats? First, check to make sure the cooling water supply is in good order. If it is an open system perhaps the intake screen has been plugged with foreign matter. Check it, the hose and pipe connections, and the water pump. If this system is in good order, check the oil level in the engine base, the

oil filter, and connecting tubing. If oil or water is not circulating
properly, try cleaning out the supply lines.

616. What is the purpose of an exhaust system?   As the name implies, this is the system on an engine that carries away the products of
combustion from the cylinders.

617. What are the principal components of an exhaust system?
After exhaust gases have passed through the exhaust valve of a cylinder
they enter the exhaust manifold, which collects the gases from all the
engine's cylinders and conveys them to the exhaust line. The latter
consists of suitably large diameter pipe which carries the hot gases to
a muffler and from there to the outer air.

Where the hot gases enter the exhaust line, water from the cooling
system is injected in an open cooling system. In a closed cooling system the exhaust line is water jacketed to keep it cool. It is important
that this line be kept cool, as overheating could cause a fire to start.

618. What is the purpose of a muffler?   As the exhaust from an internal combustion engine, if unmuffled, sounds like a rapid series of
gunshots, it is usual to prevent this objectionable noise by installing a
muffler in an exhaust system to keep it quiet.

619. Are there different kinds of mufflers?   Yes, there are many
kinds, some more effective than others. Some are water cooled, some
are dry. Some are made from welded sheet metal, others are cast iron.
All, however, provide an expansion chamber where the noise from
the engine's explosions can, to a greater or lesser degree, dissipate
their noise.

620. What is a cylinder?   It is the part of an engine in which combustion takes place and in which the piston moves up and down. Engines have been built with one, two, three, four, six, eight, twelve, and
sixteen cylinders. Inboard engines usually have one, two, four, or six
cylinders. Some engines have in-line, some have V-cylinder, arrangements, and some have a horizontally opposed cylinder arrangement.

621. How are the cylinders of an outboard motor arranged?   Outboard engines are one-, two-, or four-cylindered. Their cylinders lie

horizontally. In the two-cylinder model (called twin cylinder) the cylinders are opposed; that is, they lie opposite one another with one pushing while the other pulls. The four- and six-cylinder models are in line.

622. What is a piston?   This is the engine part, cylindrical in shape, that moves within the cylinder in which its diameter must be a very close fit. To prevent the gases of explosion from bypassing the piston it is equipped with several piston rings—flexible metal inserts which lie in slots on the piston's circumference and serve to seal the minute space between the piston and the cylinder wall.

623. How does a piston develop power?   Motion is imparted to the piston in an internal combustion engine by the explosion of a mixture of fuel and air in the combustion chamber of the cylinder. This explosion (in gasoline engines) is set off by a spark plug. To convert it into usable power the reciprocating motion of the piston must be converted to rotary motion. This is accomplished as follows: Laterally of the piston, and on its center line, is a steel rod called a wrist pin. Fitted to the wrist pin and oscillating on it is a connecting rod which, at its lower end, is connected to a crankshaft. This shaft rotates in response to impulses imparted by the connecting rod and delivers rotary motion which turns a propeller shaft to which a propeller is attached. The rotation of the propeller drives the boat.

624. What is a crankshaft?   This is the element in a reciprocating engine (gasoline, diesel, or steam) that converts reciprocating motion to rotary motion. It is interposed between the pistons (reciprocating) and the propeller shaft (rotating) and is connected to the former by means of connecting rods. The propeller shaft is coupled to the working end of the crankshaft except when the engine is equipped with reduction gears. In that case the propeller shaft is coupled to the drive shaft of the gear box.

625. What is a connecting rod?   This is the part of a reciprocating engine that acts as the connection between the piston and the crankshaft, transmitting the reciprocating motion of the piston to the rotating crankshaft.

626. What is a wrist pin? Because the reciprocating motion of a piston in a cylinder of an engine has to be translated into rotary motion of the crankshaft, a unit called a connecting rod is introduced between the two.

The part that transmits the piston's reciprocating movement to the connecting rod and permits it to oscillate is called a wrist pin. Its two ends are fixed in the piston, and it serves as the upper bearing of the connecting rod.

627. What is a cam shaft? Four-cycle gasoline engines have poppet valves, some of which admit the fuel to the cylinders and others permit the exhaust gases to escape. There are two valves to a cylinder, called intake and exhaust valves. These valves have to be opened and closed by moving up and down in their guides. The up-and-down motion is imparted by a cam shaft which rotates synchronously with the crankshaft to which it is connected by a V-belt, a chain drive, or gears.

628. What is the function of a cam? In a marine engine the function of a cam is to raise the poppet valves, one of which admits fuel to a cylinder; the other allows exhaust gases to escape.

629. What is a tappet? This is a small cylindrical device introduced in an engine between the cam shaft and the valve stem. It has an adjusting nut so that the travel or lift of the valve can be adjusted with great precision.

In engines with overhead cam shafts the tappets are between the rocker arms and the valves.

630. What is the function of a poppet valve? In a four-cycle engine there are two poppet valves to each cylinder. One admits the fuel mixture and is called an intake valve. The other allows the exhaust gases to escape and is called an exhaust valve. These valves are never open simultaneously.

631. How is a poppet valve actuated? The movement of a poppet valve is controlled by a cam and a spring. The cam opens the valve; the spring closes it.

632. What is a gear?   This is a technical term applied to a toothed wheel designed so its teeth match with another, usually of a different diameter, for the purpose of transmitting rotary motion from one shaft to another. In some cases, where gears are not in direct contact, power is delivered from one to another by a chain drive.

Perhaps the best-known example of such a drive is that between the pedals and rear wheel of a bicycle.

633. What functions do gears perform on a marine engine?   Many of the functions of an engine are set in motion by gears that receive their power from the main crankshaft. But before that shaft rotates it must be set in motion by a starter or Bendix gear, which engages teeth on the engine's flywheel to start it. Then the main shaft takes over and turns gears that operate the cooling water pump, the cam shaft that lifts the intake and exhaust valves, and the timer which delivers current to the spark plugs.

Also there are usually reverse and reduction gears between the engine and the propeller shaft. The former are for reversing the direction of rotation of the propeller shaft and propeller, thus controlling the boat's direction. Reduction gears cause the propeller shaft to turn at a slower rate than the engine's drive shaft. This arrangement permits a light, high-speed engine to deliver the same power formerly supplied by a heavy slow-speed one.

634. What purposes do bearings serve?   Every rotating part of a piece of machinery—an engine, an electric motor, a generator, or a steering gear, for example—operates within a bearing of some sort. Where high speed is involved roller bearings, needle bearings, or ball bearings are usually found. Heavier loads and slower speeds, such as those at which propeller shafts rotate, can be taken care of by bearings of bronze, Babbitt metal, or, where water-lubricated, rubber.

635. What is a crankcase?   This is the lowest part of an engine, the part encasing the crankshaft. It holds the lubricating oil into which the crankshaft dips as it revolves.

636. What purpose does a gasket serve?   Where there is any pressure on a liquid or a gas it will leak out between two flat metal surfaces no matter how carefully they may be fitted, or how tightly they may be fastened. To overcome this a gasket of softer material is introduced between the two. Such gaskets may be made of asbestos covered with a thin copper jacket, or they may be simply a piece of a special kind of paper, cork, or neoprene. The material depends on how the gasket will be used. Where it is subject to hot gases, under pressure, as between the engine block and head or between a spark plug and its seat, the asbestos-copper gasket is used. To prevent leakage of gasoline or water a neoprene or paper gasket is indicated. The neoprene gasket on the bowl of a fuel filter is an example. Between the flanges of a carburetor and an intake manifold, paper or cork is sufficient.

637. What is the function of a clutch?   This is a mechanical unit that serves as a connection between the crankshaft and the propeller shaft. When the clutch is out—that is, disengaged—the engine can run while the propeller shaft is stationary. When the clutch is in, or engaged, the propeller shaft also turns.

It consists of a smooth-faced steel member against which another part faced with a friction material called clutch lining can be pressed. When in contact the clutch is engaged. When out of contact it is disengaged. Clutches are usually operated by a foot pedal.

638. What is a stuffing box?   If it were not for a stuffing box there would be nothing to prevent water from entering a boat at the point where the propeller shaft leaves the hull and enters the water. It is a bronze fitting (or gland), attached to the hull by suitable fastenings through which the propeller shaft passes. Surrounding the shaft is waterproof packing which is kept under compression by a large nut, thus keeping out water but allowing the shaft to turn freely.

639. On a power cruiser or an auxiliary sailboat what kind of pumps will be installed?   There will be at least one bilge pump, perhaps two—one manual, one power-driven. There will be a water-circulating pump for the engine's cooling system and a fuel pump to get the fuel to the engine. There may also be an oil pump for lubricating oil. Then there will be a water pump at the galley sink (perhaps two, one for salt water) and sometimes another pump to empty the sink overboard. In the toilet room, or head, there will be a pump for basin water and another to evacuate the toilet. Big yachts usually have a special pump for hosing off the anchor as it is gotten up and for hosing down decks.

640. How are pumps classified?   There are several kinds of pumps. There are reciprocating or piston pumps in which liquid is sucked through a check valve by a piston or plunger moving in a cylinder or pump barrel, usually hand-operated. The piston must also have a check valve to allow it to be pushed down against a charge of liquid. This is the simplest form of bilge pump.

There are diaphragm pumps in which a flexible diaphragm oscillating back and forth in a chamber sucks liquid in through one valve and forces it out through another. This type of pump is used for fuel and also as a bilge pump. The fuel pump is, of course, power-operated; the bilge pump is hand operated.

Rotary pumps usually have a flexible impeller which rotates inside a circular chamber, sucking liquid in one port and forcing it out another. These also may be hand- or power-operated, and can serve as bilge pumps or for cooling water.

641. What is an hydrometer?   This is an instrument used for determining the condition of charge of a storage battery by sucking up a sample of the electrolyte in each cell. It is a glass tube about one inch in diameter and eighteen inches long, with a small orifice at one end, a rubber bulb at the other, like an oversize eye dropper. Within the tube is a small weighted glass float marked to indicate the specific gravity of the electrolyte when the latter is sucked in.

642. What is a tachometer?   This is an instrument that registers the revolutions of a shaft. On a boat it shows how fast the engine is running, the dial reading in revolutions per minute—r.p.m.

643. Why is a tachometer an important instrument?   It enables the skipper of a twin-screw vessel to synchronize the speed of his two engines. For predicted log contestants a tachometer is necessary so he can gauge his speed with pinpoint accuracy, and as an aid to navigation it helps a skipper to estimate his speed, his position, and his estimated time of arrival (ETA) with considerable assurance.

644. Why do most instrument panels include a temperature gauge thermometer? So the operator can tell at a glance if the engine is running too hot or too cold. To attain its best performance a marine engine should operate at the temperature recommended by its manufacturer.

645. Do instrument panels have more than one temperature gauge? Yes, some have two gauges for each engine—one for cooling water and one for lubricating oil.

646. Are there many types of propellers? Yes, a great many. First, there is the two-bladed wheel which is used mostly on outboard motors and by sailboats equipped with auxiliary engines. Then there is the three-bladed wheel which is popular for speedboats, power cruisers, and the larger outboards. Four-bladed propellers are mostly slow-turning wheels where extra power but not speed is required. There is a five-bladed propeller which is used on power cruisers where absence from vibration is desired.

647. How is a propeller designated? To accurately describe a propeller it is necessary to give the number of blades it has, its diameter, and its pitch.

648. What is meant by a propeller's diameter? This is the diameter of a circle that would circumscribe the propeller's blades.

649. What is meant by pitch? This is the distance a propeller would advance in making one complete revolution. This is a somewhat theoretical figure, however, as there is a certain amount of slip involved.

650. What is a propeller slip? This can be described as a propeller's efficiency factor. The greater the slip, the less the efficiency. It is the difference between the theoretical and actual advance of a propeller when making a single revolution.

651. What is meant by the term "twin screw"? This means that a boat has two complete and separate propulsion systems from starter buttons to propellers.

X. RADIOTELEPHONES
AND ELECTRICITY

Introduction. Radiotelephones are useful aboard boats for several reasons. Possibly most important, they serve as a means of calling for assistance in an emergency. Sport fishermen use them as an aid in finding fish. And they are a great convenience for sending and receiving messages when away from home port.

Marine telephone operators are located in major cities that are on or near the water. Through them a vessel at sea can call a land-based telephone anywhere in the world. By the same token, a person ashore can call a boat at sea by contacting a marine operator. In this case, however, the vessel receiving the call must be aware that it is coming, so that they will be listening to (guarding) the frequency. The operator has no way of contacting a vessel that is not listening to the proper frequency. So the vessel must call the operator to ask if there are any calls. There are also certain times at which the operator reviews the list of boats that people ashore are trying to contact.

The operation of a radiotelephone can be somewhat mystifying to the uninitiated. During a conversation only one person can talk at a time, since both parties are transmitting and receiving on the same frequency. This takes some practice, and it is a good idea to become familiar with the system.

As the radiotelephone is one of the heaviest drains on a boat's electrical supply, it is important to have at least a minimal understanding of the electrical system, and the piece of equipment using it which should always be in top operating condition.

652. How is electric current measured? Current flowing through a wire can be likened to water flowing through a pipe. It has both volume and pressure or velocity. Electric volume is expressed in amperes, velocity in volts. The combination of amperes (volume) times volts (velocity) is expressed in watts.

653. What is an ampere? This is a unit of electricity that represents the volume of current passing through a wire or conductor.

654. What is a volt? This is a measure of the pressure or velocity of an electric current passing through a wire or conductor.

655. What is a watt? This is a unit of electrical measurement that expresses the result of multiplying volts (velocity) by amperes (volume). It is the unit by which electric consumption is measured.

656. Why is it important that the correct size wire be used in a boat's electric wiring system? Oversize wiring if properly insulated is safe, but danger may exist where wire is too small to carry the load. This may cause the wire to heat up to a point where it becomes incandescent, which could ignite any explosive vapor that might be present.

Use	Wire Gage	Number Cable	Total Wire Length	Total Cable Length
Generator Circuits	12 10 8 6 5	———— ———— ————	6' or less 6' to 10' 10' to 15' 15' to 25' 25' to 50'	———— ———— ————
Starting Circuits		0 00 000	———— ————	6' or less 6' to 7-1/2' 7-1/2' to 10'
Horn Circuits	10			
Lighting Circuits	10		Note: Maximum of four 21-cp lamps per circuit	
Ignition Circuits	12 10		Note: With one coil. Note: With two coils.	
Electric Fuel Pump	12 10		Note: With one pump. Note: With two pumps.	
Remote Control Switch	12			

Electrical system wiring sizes

657. What determines the size of wire required for a boat's electric system? This depends on the voltage of the boat's electrical system, the total wattage of each fixture in the circuit, and the length of wire between the most distant one and the current source.

658. Is there any non-dangerous result from undersize wiring? Yes, such wiring, by failing to supply sufficient current to a fixture, such as a light, will cause it to give out less illumination than required of it.

659. How can one detect the location of a faulty electrical fixture or connection?   By the use of a voltmeter or a test lamp. If one contact of the meter or lamp is connected to ground, the flow of current can be detected by testing with the other lead or contact. By testing the various terminals in a circuit the faulty one will be revealed when the meter fails to register or the lamp to light.

660. What is meant by "short circuit"?   As one side of a wiring system is connected to ground, if any part of it, such as a fixture or a connection, becomes defective it can cause a short circuit. This means that instead of following its normal course from battery or generator through the various devices in the circuit, the current is being routed to ground without performing any useful work and is in fact out of control.

661. What symptoms indicate a short circuit?   A fixture, such as a lamp, may fail to operate when the switch is turned, indicating that current is not flowing properly. This may be caused by a lamp blowing or by corroded contacts. But a short can also develop due to broken or disconnected wiring which makes contact with another object that is in contact with ground. This condition can be very dangerous and should be corrected at once.

662. What action is required if a short circuit develops?   In properly installed wiring there should be fuses or circuit breakers to protect each wiring circuit, which will "blow" if a short circuit develops. But if there are no fuses and there is a master switch in the wiring system (and there should be), throw it to "open" at once. If there is no such switch, disconnect the battery.

663. Is a short circuit dangerous?   It can be very dangerous. Not only will it drain the battery, but if sufficient current is present, it can cause wires to heat up to a point where fire breaks out. Or perhaps, if a wire is disconnected or broken, a spark may jump the gap which, if any gasoline or cooking gas fumes are present, can cause an explosion.

664. How does one compute the amperage load in a given circuit?
Total the wattage of the various devices to be serviced by the circuit and divide this total by the voltage available. For example, a total load of 150 watts in a 12-volt system would require a wire capacity of 13 amperes:

$$\frac{150}{12} = 12.5$$

665. What is meant by the term "polarity"? This is an electrical term meaning the direction in which current flows.

666. Are pleasure craft required to carry radio telephones? No, but if they do, they must comply with FCC regulations.

667. What are the basic FCC rules to be observed when operating a radiophone?
1. Only the holder of a license or permit should operate the set.
2. On the marine band, keep the set tuned to 2182 kc. during standby time (the international calling and distress frequency).
3. Keep a record (called a log) of every call.
4. On citizen's band channels maintain a conelrad standby; no log is required of this, however.
5. Use no improper language.
6. Don't repeat what you may overhear, nor take advantage of it.
7. Don't send unnecessary, false, or deceptive signals.
8. Identify each call by giving your own call sign.
9. Don't talk unnecessarily, and not for longer than five minutes.

668. Is a license required to operate a marine band radiophone?
Yes, two licenses: a Station License and a Restricted Radiotelephone Operator Permit.

If you plan to use a transceiver to contact licensed radiophone units, you must apply for a Station License, otherwise no license is required for transceivers.

669. What are the requirements to get a Restricted Radiophone Operator Permit? The applicant must be a United States citizen and be able to write, speak, and understand English. He must also be familiar with the treaties, laws, rules, and regulations affecting permit holders.

670. Is there a penalty for making false statements when applying for a Restricted Radiotelephone Operator Permit? Yes. Five years in prison or $10,000 fine or both is the penalty for making false statements.

671. According to FCC regulations, who may legally speak over a radiophone? Anyone may speak, but the contact must be made by the person holding the operator's permit.

672. What are the responsibilities of a holder of a Restricted Radiotelephone Operator Permit? He is entirely responsible for the operation of his station. Only he can make contact with other stations. He must also supervise transmission if another uses the phone, keep a regulation radio log, and sign off when the conversation is over.

673. Where does one get a copy of the FCC rules for operating a radiophone? The FCC rules and regulations that apply to a given service can be had from the Superintendent of Documents, Government Printing Office, Washington 25, D.C.

Some manufacturers supply copies of the FCC rules to customers gratis, but the government makes a charge, which varies according to service covered.

674. How much do the FCC rules and regulations cost? This depends on which part is required. They are divided thus:

Marine radiotelephone—FCC Rules, Part 8, Volume 4, $2.50
Citizen's band—Part 19, Volume 6, $1.25
Very low power transceivers—Part 15, Volume 2, $2.00

675. How is an FCC station license obtained? The dealer from whom a set is bought will usually supply an FCC application form. This must be filled out by the owner of the set, notarized, and sent to the FCC.

676. Is a station license required in order legally to operate a radiophone? Yes. The law requires that before a phone goes on the air a license be obtained from the Federal Communications Commission

(FCC). This applies to sets of over 0.1 watt capacity. Transceivers of less than 0.1 watt capacity need no license unless they are to be used to contact licensed equipment. In that case a license is required.

677. How long does it take to get a Marine Radiotelephone Station license? It may take as long as two months after application is made.

678. Is an interim license available? Yes. An interim ship station license can be procured by applying in person (the owner or a representative) to an FCC Field Engineering Office.

679. What is the fee for an FCC radiophone station license? There is no fee.

680. Are radio technicians licensed? To be a qualified radio technician a man must hold a second class (or higher) license, issued by the FCC. Only a licensed technician is permitted by law to tune or to make adjustments on transmitters.

681. What is the source of power for a radiophone? Usually radiophones derive their power from the battery that operates the starter. Some boats, however, have separate batteries for lights and electrical equipment; in such cases it is usual to hook up the radiophone to this current source.

The capacity (ampere-hours) of the battery determines the size radiophone that can be satisfactorily operated. A competent specialist should be consulted before making purchases of equipment.

682. How much power is required by a radiophone? Standard marine radiophones range in power from 15 to 30 watts for the smallest to 150 watts, or even more, for the most powerful.

683. How many channels (band frequencies) should a radiophone have? From three to five.

684. What are the channels?
International distress frequency 2182 kc.
Ship-to-ship 2638 kc.
Ship-to-shore kc. (according to area)

Coast Guard   2670 kc.
Second ship-to-shore   2738 kc.

These channels are pretuned and are precisely controlled by crystals. Some radiophones will also pick up the standard broadcast bands.

685. How is radiophone power rated?   Transmitter power is subject to strict regulation by the FCC and is rated in "input watts," referred to usually simply as watts.

686. What is an input watt?   This is the measure of the power of a transmitter. The greater the power, the longer the range. However, the exact distance a radiophone will transmit cannot be accurately predicted. Static affects the range. So do the time of day, the efficiency of the installation, and other factors.

A rough rule of thumb is that a radiophone should transmit on marine frequencies a minimum of one mile per input watt. And, under favorable conditions, the range may be greater.

687. Does a radiophone affect the ship's compass?   Yes. It should be located not less than three feet from the compass.

688. Does a radiophone require special wiring?   As the set makes a fairly heavy drain on its battery when in use, it is unwise to connect it into existing lighting or other low amperage circuit. A radiophone should have its own wiring direct to the battery. The cable should be as short as possible and of sufficient size so there is no voltage drop. Cables should be securely anchored and protected from moisture or mechanical damage.

A fuse or circuit breaker should be installed in the hot lead near the battery.

689. What is the best location for a radiophone?   First, it should be at least three feet away from the ship's compass; it should be well sheltered from the elements, and it should be handy to the helmsman or the skipper. But don't have it in a location where passers by may bump it. The set should be securely fastened down yet accessible for servicing—and protect it from vibration. Try to locate the set so all wiring can be kept as short as possible, particularly the antenna and ground wires.

690. What precautions are advisable when locating an antenna?
It should be so located that there is no danger of its being damaged, and
it should not be used as a handhold. The mountings should be well
fastened.

691. How high should a radiophone antenna be?   The higher the
better. The efficiency of the set's performance depends largely on having a suitable antenna. On a small powerboat, 12 feet would be about
right, but 18 feet or more is recommended for larger boats. Sailboats
sometimes use an insulated backstay as an antenna.

692. Does lightning sometimes strike an antenna?   Yes, occasionally.

**693. What precautions against lightning should be observed when
installing an antenna?**   The base of the antenna should be grounded
by means of a heavy wire (not less than 8 gauge) to the boat's largest
underwater metal object. At the bottom of the antenna, connected to
the ground cable, a suitable lightning arrestor should be installed.

**694. Is it advisable to remove a radiophone and other electronic
gear from a boat when she is out of commission?**   Yes. Such eqiup-
ment should be checked by a competent serviceman and stored in a
dry place during the time a boat is out of commission. Corrosion and
dampness should be avoided if electronic gear is to function satisfactorily. Several bags of silica gel, sold in hardware stores under
various names, should be hung near the equipment during storage to
prevent dampness.

695. What can be done to reduce engine noise in a radiophone?
Noise suppressors or ignition shielding must be installed around
the engine if satisfactory reception is to be expected when the engine
is running. Spark gaps cause noise in earphones, but this can be reduced by shielding.

696. What is shielding?   This is a system of suppressing radio noise
caused by the spark gaps when an engine is running. A shielding system can be installed by an amateur, but usually it is better to have a
professional do the work.

697. Does a radiophone have to be grounded?   Yes. It is usual to connect the set to a ground plate on the outside of the hull, below the waterline, usually near the keel. This can be a sheet of copper of suitable size and thickness, connected to the set with a heavy-gauge wire. The ground plate is important if satisfactory transmission is to be attained.

698. What is a citizen's band radiophone?   This is a low-powered instrument, limited by the Federal Communications Commission (FCC) to 5 watts, and has a theoretical maximum range of 15–20 miles, but don't count on this. Actually transmission may be good for only a mile or two. It is also called a transceiver.

699. How useful is a transceiver or citizen's band radiophone? For certain purposes it can be very useful. Communication between home, club, or other boats can be carried on for short distances, and in some areas specific channels (channel 13 is often suggested) have been assigned for boatman's use.

As there are no government stations tuned to these frequencies, you cannot contact such facilities.

700. What power source is required for citizen's band transceivers?   They can be had to operate on AC shore current or on 6- or 12-volt batteries.

Very low powered sets (less than 0.1 watt) are suitable for short distances. They have hand-held transmitters with self-contained batteries and can be used for talking from boat to boat for a mile or two.

701. How many bands or frequencies are available for citizen's band radiophones (transceivers)?   The FCC has assigned 23 bands to this use, and any band may be used.

702. Other than its low power, what determines the range of a citizen's band radiophone?   The height of the antenna, which is limited by the FCC to 20 feet, and the local conditions. Over water 15 to 20 miles is theoretically possible. Where local interference exists, distance may be reduced to a mile or two.

XI. NAVIGATION

Introduction. Navigation is one of the arts essential to the repertoire of the complete seaman. Knowledge of navigation and the ability to put it to practical use will allow a yachtsman of limited experience to cross a protected body of water by day, or, should his skills advance to that extent, a great ocean.

Much credit for the early development of navigation is given Prince Henry the Navigator, a fifteenth-century Portuguese patron of exploration who established a famous observatory and school for navigators at Sagres.

703. What is the "General Prudence Rule" of navigation? This rule says "nothing shall exonerate any vessel, or owner . . . from the consequences of failure to take any precaution which may be required by the ordinary practice of seamen or the special circumstances of the case."

704. Is there more than one kind of navigation? Yes. There are celestial navigation, dead reckoning, and piloting. Also there is navigation by using such modern electronic aids as radar, loran, sonar, radio direction finder (RDF), etc.

705. What is celestial navigation? This is the art of finding the position of a vessel by taking sights on heavenly bodies.

706. What is meant by dead reckoning (DR)? This is a method of navigation based on a carefully kept record of time, course, drift, and speed. These elements are noted in a log (log book) and, if properly recorded, enable the navigator to fix his position at any moment with considerable accuracy. In fact, before the days of radio direction finders and Loran, it was not unusual for trans-Atlantic liners, when the weather was bad, to cross the ocean and make their landfalls by dead reckoning alone.

707. What is the origin of the term "dead reckoning"? It is a corruption of the expression "deduced reckoning" which was often abbre-

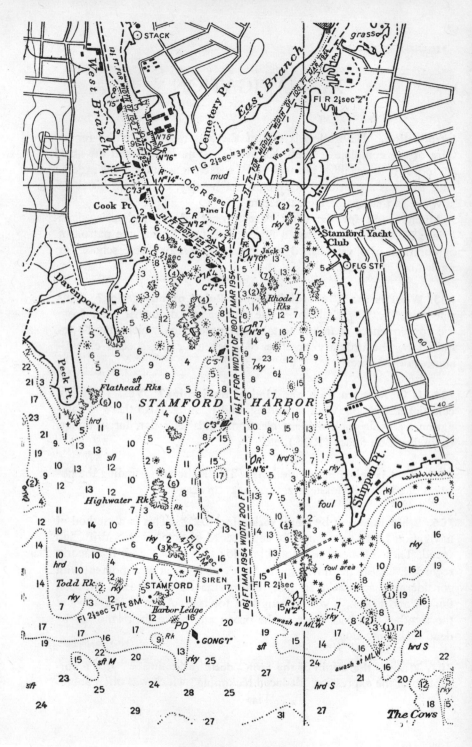

Section of a typical chart

viated in log books as "ded. rec." It is customary now to abbreviate it as DR.

708. What is piloting? This is finding one's position on a chart by the use of DR, visual sightings of aids to navigation and soundings.

709. What do charts show? Charts, together with related publications, furnish the information necessary for safe navigation. They show depths and bottom characteristics, dangers, channels, landmarks, aids to navigation, fish trap limits, restricted, prohibited, cable, and pipeline areas, wharves, cities, and many other important details.

710. What charts are published by the U.S. Coast and Geodetic Survey? The Coast and Geodetic Survey publishes coastal and harbor charts and related publications of the United States and its possessions.

711. Where may Coast and Geodetic Survey charts be purchased? At USC&GS offices in New York, San Francisco, and Washington, or from authorized nautical chart agents located throughout the country.

712. What is the plane of reference for charts? The plane of reference for water depths on Coast and Geodetic Survey charts is mean low water. The effect of strong winds in combination with regular tidal action may at times cause the water level to rise or fall considerably below the reference plane.

713. How can you tell if a Coast and Geodetic Survey chart is up to date? The number of the chart and the edition date, sometimes followed by revision date, are printed on the lower left corner of the chart. New editions cancel all former editions. Charts may be corrected from local or weekly "Notices to Mariners" published subsequent to the stamped date to which the chart is corrected.

714. What charts are available from the U.S. Navy Oceanographic (formerly Hydrographic) Office? Nautical charts of the entire world except for the United States and its possessions are available from the USN Oceanographic Office. Mostly, these are published by the Oceanographic Office, but some are produced by foreign nations.

715. How may Oceanographic Office charts and publications be purchased? Whenever possible these charts and publications should be purchased from a local authorized sales agent. They may also be purchased from local branch Oceanographic Offices or by mail from the USN Oceanographic Office, Washington 25, D.C. A list of charts and their prices may be obtained at the above address. Mail orders should be accompanied by a check or money order in the proper amount.

716. How are Coast and Geodetic Survey conventional charts classified? They are broken down into four types—harbor charts, coast charts, general charts, and sailing charts.

Intracoastal waterway charts, which used to be of the conventional type, have been converted to the small-craft series format.

717. What are harbor charts? Harbor charts are intended for navigation and anchorage in harbors and small waterways. The exact scale used depends on the size and importance of the harbor and the existing dangers, but it is normally about 0.7 miles per inch.

718. What are coast charts? Coast charts are for navigation inside offshore reefs and shoals, entering bays and harbors of considerable size, and on certain inland waterways. Scale is approximately 1.4 miles to the inch.

719. What are general charts? General charts, with a scale of approximately 8.2 miles to the inch, are for use when a vessel's position is well offshore but can still be fixed by visual observation of landmarks, lights, buoys, and characteristic soundings.

720. What are C&GS sailing charts? Sailing charts are plotting charts used for offshore navigation between distant coastal ports and for approaching the coast from the open ocean. Scales are often the same as general charts.

721. How are Coast and Geodetic Survey small-craft charts classified and how are they different from conventional charts? The letters SC following chart numbers designate charts published with special small-craft information which conventional charts do not have, such as docking facilities, supplies, services, tides, and currents printed on the chart or on its protective cover. These charts are assigned to one of three groups.

722. What is the first group of Coast and Geodetic Survey small-craft charts? Group I small-craft charts (numbered 100-SC to 199-SC) are chart folios consisting of three or four folded sheets printed front and back and bound in a cover.

723. What are Group II C&GS small-craft charts? The charts numbered 600-SC to 699-SC are route charts of rivers and narrow waterways. They consist of a folded single sheet printed front and back and inserted in a jacket.

Charts numbered 800-SC to 899-SC come in the same form as above and are route charts of the intracoastal waterway.

724. What are Group III C&GS small-craft charts? These are numbered 70-SC to 9500-SC and are area charts that do not include Groups I and II. They are generally conventional charts with additional information for small boats. They come folded into convenient panels and are issued in a protective cover.

725. How often are new editions of small-craft charts published? Unlike conventional charts, new editions of small-craft charts are published annually on a regular basis and cancel all former editions. The number and the date of the edition are printed on the lower left corner of each chart page. Changes between editions must be made from local or weekly "Notices to Mariners."

726. What charts are published by the U.S. Lake Survey? Charts of Lake Champlain, Oneida Lake, New York State Barge Canals, the St. Lawrence River above St. Regis and Cornwall, the Great Lakes, and Minnesota-Ontario Border Lakes.

They are available from the U.S. Lake Survey, 630 Federal building, Detroit, Michigan, and its authorized agents.

727. Who publishes and sells charts of the Ohio River and its tributaries? U.S. Engineer Office, Cincinnati, Ohio.

728. What charts are published by the Mississippi River Commission? Charts of the Mississippi River from its source to the delta. They may be obtained from the Secretary, Mississippi River Commission, Vicksburg, Mississippi.

729. Who publishes charts of Canadian coastal and Great Lakes waters? The Canadian Hydrographic Service, Ottawa, Canada, publishes the above charts.

730. What charts are published by the U.S. Engineer Office in Chicago, Illinois? Charts of Illinois waterways, Lake Michigan to the Mississippi River, and the Mississippi from Cairo, Illinois, to Minneapolis, Minnesota.

731. Who publishes the light lists for United States waters? The U.S. Coast Guard. They are available from the Superintendent of Documents, Government Printing Office, Washington 25, D.C., and authorized Coast Guard sales agents, who are normally the same as those who sell charts.

732. What are "Notices to Mariners"? This is a weekly pamphlet prepared by the U.S. Coast Guard, USN Oceanographic Office, and the C&GS. They are issued free by the Oceanographic Office to anybody who wants them. They are intended as a safety aid and list changes so that charts and related publications may be kept up to date.

733. What are "Local Notices to Mariners"? "Local Notices to Mariners" are issued by each Coast Guard district and should be used in place of the weekly "Notice to Mariners" when operating within the confines of one particular Coast Guard district.

734. What are "Coast Pilots"? These are volumes published by the Coast and Geodetic Survey primarily to furnish navigators with information that cannot conveniently be shown on charts and is not readily available elsewhere. They contain general information about the weather, coast, harbors, port facilities, and sailing directions.

735. What areas are covered by C&GS "Coast Pilots"?   The coast and harbors of the continental United States, Alaska, Puerto Rico, and the Virgin Islands are covered by the various "Coast Pilot" volumes.

736. What are the five "Coast Pilot" volumes?
Vol. 1—Atlantic Coast, Sec. A, Eastport, Me., to Cape Cod, Mass.
Vol. 2—Atlantic Coast, Sec. B, Cape Cod, Mass., to Sandy Hook, N.J.
Vol. 3—Sandy Hook, N.J., to Cape Henry, Va.
Vol. 4—Cape Henry, Va., to Key West, Fla.
Vol. 5—Gulf Coast, Puerto Rico, and Virgin Islands.

737. How are "Coast Pilots" kept up to date?   Supplements are normally issued early each year which are complete and cancel all previous issues. They contain changes reported from date of edition and are free of charge.

738. How often are new editions of "Coast Pilots" published?   A new edition of "Coast Pilots" is published about every seven years, but the interval may vary from five to twelve years depending upon the importance of the region and other factors.

739. How much do "Coast Pilots" cost?   Each volume sells for $2.50.

740. What are "Tide Tables"?   This is an annual publication of the U.S. Coast and Geodetic Survey that gives predictions of the times and heights of high and low waters for every day in the year at many of the more important harbors. Differences for calculating predictions at numerous other places are also given.

741. What are "Tidal Current Tables"?   This is another annual C&GS publication that gives daily predictions of the times of slack water and the times and velocities of maximum flood and ebb currents for numerous waterways. Differences for calculating predictions at many additional locations are included.

742. What are "Tidal Current Charts"? These are a set of twelve charts which depict, by arrows and figures, the direction and velocity of tidal current for each hour of the tidal cycle. The charts are good for any year, and present a comprehensive view of the tidal current movement in the locality as a whole. The charts are used with the "Tidal Current Tables" except for the New York Harbor charts, which must be used with the "Tide Tables."

743. What is *Eldridge*? This is a tide and pilot book which is published annually. It contains in one 200-page volume a great deal of information useful to yachtsmen in waters between Maine and Chesapeake Bay.

744. How may a copy of *Eldridge* be obtained? In the areas served by the book, many marine supply houses and nautical bookstores carry it. Or it may be ordered by direct mail for $2.00 from the publisher: Robert Eldridge White, 178 Atlantic Avenue, Boston, Massachusetts 02110.

745. What is a rhumb line? This is the most direct line between two points. In open water with nothing between, it would be either a straight or great-circle course.

746. What is a great circle course? A great circle course is the shortest distance between two widely separated points taking into account the curvature of the earth.

747. What is the color code on channel buoys? Aids to navigation that mark the starboard side of a channel when entering from seaward are red, those to port are black. In other words: red, right, returning; black, right, out.

748. What is the numbering system on channel buoys? Red aids to navigation are even-numbered and black aids are odd-numbered. They run in sequence toward land.

749. What is the meaning of a red-and-black aid to navigation? These aids mark the junction of channels or underwater obstructions. Like black-and-white aids they carry no numbers.

nun (red)
even number

can (black)
odd number

spar (red or black)
even or odd number

obstruction buoys
(red & black)

fairway buoys (black & white)

small lighted buoys (red or black)
even or odd number

beacons
obstruction

channel marker

Types of buoys

750. What does a black-and-white aid to navigation indicate?
This is a midchannel marker and is not numbered.

751. How are channel lights color coded? Red aids to navigation
show red lights, while black aids show white or green lights.

752. What is the difference between a flashing light and an occulting light? Flashing lights blink on at intervals, whereas occulting lights blink off at intervals. Occulting lights, therefore, are lit for considerably more time than flashing lights.

753. What is the meaning of visibility distances given for lights on charts and in the light lists?   The distances at which lights may be seen in clear weather are geographic ranges computed in nautical miles for a height of the observer's eye of 15 feet above sea level. In cases where lights are not of sufficient candlepower to be seen to the limit of their geographic ranges, the luminous ranges are given.

754. In observing navigational lights from a distance, what precaution should be taken?   The distance of an observer from a light cannot be estimated by its apparent intensity, and care should be taken to avoid trying to do so. Powerful lights in the distance can easily be confused with nearby lights of similar characteristics.

Also, the apparent characteristics of a complex light may change with the distance of the observer. The proper characteristic may not be recognized until nearer the light. In a heavy sea, a light may alternately appear and disappear, giving a false characteristic.

755. How close may lights be passed?   Lighthouses and beacons should never be passed close aboard. In many cases rip-rap mounds are maintained to protect them against ice and water damage.

756. What should you do if you observe a discrepancy in an aid to navigation?   Promptly notify the nearest Coast Guard District Commander if an aid to navigation is observed to be missing, sunk, capsized, out of position, damaged, extinguished, or showing improper characteristics.

757. What is a diaphone?   This is the signal-producing equipment of such navigational aids as lightships and lighthouses. The diaphone signal has two tones, the second always being lower than the first.

758. How do intracoastal waterway aids to navigation differ from all others?   Intracoastal waterway aids to navigation have yellow borders or bands not found on buoys in other locations.

759. What are responsibilities of the U.S. Army Corps of Engineers?   The Army Engineers have charge of the improvement of rivers and harbors and miscellaneous other civil works, including the administration of federal laws for the preservation and protection of navigable waters, the approval of bridge plans, and the removal of sunken vessels that endanger navigation. A great deal of their time is devoted to the intracoastal waterway.

760. What is the origin of the expression "Down East" with reference to the Maine coast? Sailing ships sailed "downwind" with the prevailing SW wind, when making their easting from ports to the westward; hence the expression.

761. What purposes does the liquid in a compass bowl serve? This liquid serves two purposes: it damps or steadies the motion of the card, and it also tends to float the card so that a minimum weight rests on its pivot or bearing, thus reducing wear and prolonging the useful life of the instrument.

762. What liquid is used in a marine compass bowl? Inferior instruments are filled with oil, but a standard compass is filled with a liquid consisting of a mixture of 45 percent alcohol and 55 percent distilled water.

763. What are gimbals? Gimbals consist of a nonmagnetic metal ring, usually brass, which has four pivot points or trunnions—two points arranged parallel to the center line of the ship and two points at 90 degrees from them. The compass body is suspended in trunnions from one pair while the ring is suspended from the other pair.

764. How does a mariner's compass differ from other kinds? It is invariably a liquid compass and is usually mounted in gimbals.

765. What purpose do gimbals serve on a compass? They permit the compass to remain level regardless of the motion of the boat.

766. What is a compass card? This is the vital part of the instrument that remains stationary in relation to the earth while the boat and, of course, the compass move about it. It is circular in form and carries on its edges the degrees and/or the points of the compass.

767. How does a compass card function? At its center a compass card has a bearing (usually jeweled) which rests on a pointed pivot about which it is free to turn with minimum friction. It also carries a magnet, which is the heart of the instrument. As it is the nature of a magnet, if it is free to turn, to point to the north magnetic pole, it can be seen that when suspended on a jeweled bearing and floating in a liquid it will always remain stationary in relation to the pole.

768. How does the phenomenon of the magnet serve yachtsmen? By always enabling him to orient the bearing of his vessel with the magnetic pole, by use of a compass, he knows in what direction his vessel is headed.

769. What is a lubber line? On the forward edge of the compass body, or bowl, and in alignment with the boat's center line, is a mark, or on some compasses a wire, usually white, which indicates the direction in which the boat's bow is pointing in relation to the compass card. On some compasses there are two, sometimes four, lubber lines. In the first they are 180 degrees apart—in other words, the second one indicates the stern. When there are four they are 90 degrees apart, the two extras indicating the port and starboard beam of the boat.

770. What purpose do the extra lubber lines on a compass serve? These extra lines are uesful in taking bearings on objects such as other vessels or landmarks—a lighthouse, for example. They can also be helpful to a helmsman in his job of steering the boat if, for any reason, the forward lubber line is not easy to see.

771. What is a binnacle? This is the name of the housing in which a compass is mounted.

772. Are binnacles on sail and power boats the same? Usually on sailboats longer than, say, 35 feet overall, the binnacle is a cylindrical brass box mounted on a tubular pedestal to bring the compass to a convenient height for the helmsman. On powerboats of the larger sizes, the binnacle may also be a cylindrical brass box but without a pedestal, as it is mounted directly on the shelf forward of the steering wheel.

On smaller boats, both sail and power, there usually is no binnacle, the compass being mounted in a simple portable box.

773. What is meant by boxing the compass? Naming the points and quarter-points, beginning at north and proceeding clockwise, is called boxing the compass.

774. Can any compass be boxed? No, only one whose card is marked in points. If the card is graduated only in degrees it cannot be boxed.

775. How are the cards of most modern boat compasses marked? The most popular marking is in both points and degrees.

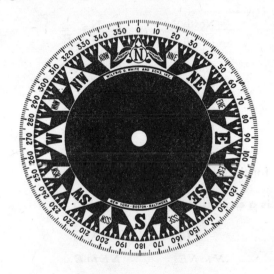

A mariner's compass card

776. How many points are there on a compass card? Thirty-two.

777. How many degrees are there on a compass card? Three hundred and sixty.

778. How many degrees are there to one point? To find this figure, divide 360 by 32. The answer is 11¼ degrees to a point.

779. What are the cardinal points of a compass? North (0°), east (90°), south (180°), and west (270°) are the cardinal points.

780. What are the intercardinal points of a compass? Northeast (NE, 45°); southeast (SE, 135°); southwest (SW, 225°) and northwest (NW, 315°).

781. How are the points between cardinal and intercardinal points designated? The midpoint between N and NE is NNE and between NE and E it is ENE—and so on in each quadrant.

782. How are the abbreviations for the points of a compass written?

North	N
North by east	N × E
North northeast	NNE
Northeast by north	NE × N
Northeast	NE
Northeast by east	NE × E
East northeast	ENE
East by north	E × N
East	E

And so on, for the other three quadrants.

783. How is a compass boxed?   (× = by)

FIRST QUADRANT

N to NE	*NE to E*
N	NE
N ¼ E	NE ¼ E
N ½ E	NE ½ E
N ¾ E	NE ¾ E
N × E	NE × E
N × E ¼ E	NE × E ¼ E
N × E ½ E	NE × E ½ E
N × E ¾ E	NE × E ¾ E
NNE	ENE
NNE ¼ E	ENE ¼ E
NNE ½ E	ENE ½ E
NNE ¾ E	ENE ¾ E
NE × N	E × N

NE ¾ N	E ¾ N
NE ½ N	E ½ N
NE ¼ N	E ¼ N
NE	E

The other three quadrants follow in this order.

784. Are the north magnetic pole and the true or geographic north pole in the same location on the earth? No. The magnetic pole is some distance from the geographic pole.

785. Where is the magnetic pole in relation to the true north pole? It is in a position between Hudson's Bay and the geographic pole.

786. Is the magnetic pole stationary? No, it moves very slowly in a small circle.

787. What is meant by deviation? When a compass is installed in a boat, particularly a powerboat or an auxiliary, there is usually enough iron or steel present near the compass to affect its magnet with the result that the compass card will not point accurately to the magnetic north. This phenomenon is called deviation. It can be caused by the proximity of an engine, for example.

788. Can deviation of a compass be corrected? Yes. It is possible to remove all or most deviation by the use of compensating magnets.

789. Can compass deviation be corrected by an amateur? If the deviation is serious it is wiser to have the compass corrected by a professional, as it is a tricky business.

790. Of what use is a deviation table? This is a point-by-point record of the deviation of a particular compass, left in its fixed position, after it has been corrected. As it frequently is impossible to correct a compass so it reads perfectly on all points of steering, it is customary to make a list or table showing what course must be steered according to the ship's compass in order to make good a desired actual course. For example, to make good a course of E mag. (east magnetic) it may be necessary to steer E ½ S (east, a half south) by ship's compass.

If one uses degrees instead of points, the foregoing example would read—course to be made good 90° magnetic; course to steer by ship's compass 96°. Actually, ½ point is 5.6-plus degrees, but a helmsman can't hold a course as close as a fraction of a degree, so the nearest full degree is steered.

791. What is meant by variation? This term is applied to the difference in location between the true north pole and the magnetic north pole.

792. Does variation change from year to year? Yes. As the north magnetic pole keeps moving in a small circle its position relative to the true north pole is constantly changing to a minute degree.

793. What is the effect of change in variation on the compass roses printed on charts? Annual change in variation gradually introduces an error in the magnetic compass roses on charts. They are replotted on every new edition if the error is appreciable. The amount and date of variation and the amount of annual change are printed with the compass rose.

794. What is a pelorus? This is an instrument used for taking relative bearings from a fixed position on a vessel. It is also called a dumb compass.

It consists of a fixed ring which has a zero mark, or lubber line, set exactly in line with the center line of the vessel. This ring is mounted in gimbals. It also has a compass card, pivoted at its center, which can be moved manually so it lies in exactly the same direction as the ship's compass.

A pair of sighting vanes are mounted on a movable arm, which also is pivoted at the center of the pelorus. These vanes can be moved independently of the card and are used to sight through at an object (say another vessel) whose relative bearing is desired.

795. Is it important that the compass card of the pelorus be in exact agreement with the vessel's compass card when taking a bearing? Yes, they must agree or an allowance for difference must be made.

796. How is a bearing taken with a pelorus? The sighting vanes are erected and a sight taken (looking through the slot) of the object whose bearing is desired. The movable compass card should first be set to agree with the ship's compass, and when the sight is taken the angle between the ship's course and the bearing is recorded. After applying the known variation of the ship's compass for the course steered, the reciprocal bearing (magnetic) gives a line of position with respect to the observed object.

797. What is a hand-bearing compass? This is a small portable magnetic compass having sighting vanes and a prism for reading bearings. It has a handle attached below its bowl usually containing flashlight batteries so that the compass card can be illuminated for taking night bearings. With a hand-bearing compass sights can be taken from any position that commands a view of the sighted object, but care must be taken not to stand close to any metal which might affect the compass card.

798. What is a bow and beam bearing and what purpose does it serve? The purpose in taking such bearings is to determine the distance-off a vessel passes the sighted object—a point of land, for example.

As the vessel approaches the object to be sighted, set the vanes of a pelorus or a bearing circle at 45 degrees to its lubber line. When the object lines up in the vanes, note the exact course and time. Realign the vanes at 90 degrees to the lubber line and take a second sight when the object lines up in the vanes. Again note the time. Figure the elapsed time between the two bearings and apply it to the speed the vessel is making over the bottom. The result will equal the distance-off from the observed object. For example: Time of first sight 12:35. Time of second sight, 12:55. Speed made good of vessel, 12 m.p.h. Then $12:55 - 12:35 = 20$ min. $\frac{20}{60} \times 12 = 4$. This vessel is 4 miles off the point.

799. What is a cross bearing? This is a means of fixing the location of a vessel by taking at least two bearings on fixed objects whose position is known. In celestial navigation this would be two stars. In long-shore navigation it could be any prominent landmarks whose positions are shown on a chart. The objects should be as nearly at right angles from the vessel as possible. When the bearing of each is determined by means of a pelorus, hand-bearing compass, or radio direction finder the reciprocals of the bearings are plotted on the chart, and where they cross is the vessel's location.

800. Why would a navigator want to take horizontal sextant sights? To ascertain his distance from two known landmarks—a lighthouse and a water tower, for example. As such marks are recorded on nautical charts, a navigator can calculate his distance offshore by measuring the angle between them and laying it out on the chart. His position will be determined by taking a compass bearing on one of the marks. He can also determine his position by taking cross bearings.

801. What does reciprocal mean? The reciprocal of a bearing is the opposite direction or 180 degrees away from the observed angle. Suppose a bearing is taken on a lighthouse which bears 45 degrees from the vessel. Then the reciprocal would be 45 degrees plus 180 degrees or 225 degrees. This would be how the vessel bears *from the light-house*. This is the information a navigator needs to determine his position.

802. What is meant by averaging the course? As a practical matter a helmsman cannot hold a vessel to a perfect compass course because of the effect of wind and waves on the vessel's hull which tend to cause her to wander off course. Experienced helmsmen know this and therefore make a practice of compensating for a swing to one side by a corresponding swing to the opposite side of the proper course, thus averaging the course.

803. What equipment does a celestial navigator need to take a sight? He uses a sextant to determine the angle between the horizon and the heavenly body (star, moon, or sun) on which he is taking a sight.

He also must have a stopwatch (or equivalent), a chronometer or a reliable radio receiver, and reference tables.

804. What is a sextant? This is a highly accurate scientific instrument used by a navigator for measuring the angle between a heavenly body and the horizon. As it measures angles, a sextant is also useful in determining the horizontal angle between known landmarks. It can also be used to approximate a ship's distance from a mark (a lighthouse, for example) whose height is known.

805. How does a navigator identify a star? A beginner may refer to a star chart of the heavens, but an experienced navigator gets to know the usual stars on which sights are taken.

806. Do navigators take sights on any heavenly body? No, only on those whose positions are listed in the tables to which they refer.

807. What is a chronometer? This is a clock used by navigators to keep track of Greenwich time. It was perfected in 1773 by John Harrison, a Yorkshire carpenter who received a reward of twenty thousand pounds from King George III after much delay. Prior to the invention of the chronometer navigators had no reliable means of keeping track of time. A chronometer may not record the exact time at Greenwich, but it must have a constant and known daily gain or loss and is "rated" accordingly. This rate is one of the factors a navigator must take into account when figuring his position from sights on celestial bodies.

808. Why do navigators use Greenwich civil time (GCT) in their calculations? Greenwich, England, is located exactly on the zero meridian of longitude, and all tables and many other calculations are based on this meridian.

809. How may time signals be obtained at sea? The National Bureau of Standards broadcasts time signals from its radio station WWV near Washington, D.C., on radio frequencies of 2.5, 5, 10, 15, 20, and 25 megacycles which are on the air 24 hours a day.

810. How does a navigator take a sight? First he locates the heavenly body (star, moon, or sun) in the small telescope of his sextant; then by moving the arm of the instrument (which carries a small mirror) he brings the reflection of the body down to the horizon. Only the lower "limb" (the bottom edge) of the heavenly body should appear to touch the horizon. The instant this feat is accomplished is noted from his stopwatch, and the angle recorded by the sextant at that time also is recorded. This procedure is repeated several times on each body sighted. The average of the series of sights is figured and taken as a "fix," or the ship's position.

811. How many sights does a navigator take to find his position?
He usually takes several sights on each selected heavenly body, noting the exact time with his stopwatch, and the angle recorded by the sextant. Sights will be taken on several stars—preferably at wide distances apart—in order to get cross bearings.

812. After sights have been recorded, what does a navigator do next? He works up his sights by referring to the printed tables which give him the exact position of the heavenly bodies on which sights have been taken. He also must refer to an accurate timing device, a chronometer or radio time signals, to determine Greenwich mean time (GMT). The difference between local time and GMT gives the navigator his position east or west of Greenwich, which is on the zero-degree meridian of longitude.

813. How accurately should a navigator be able to fix his vessel's position by celestial navigation. A navigator should be able to fix a vessel's position at sea within a few miles. Normally, his sights will form a small triangle, and he will take its center as his fix. This is the accepted means of averaging the error.

814. How can the navigator's shipmates be of help to him when he is taking sights? By recording the times and instrument readings as they are called by the navigator, a helper frees him to concentrate on the accuracy of his sights. As the motion of a small boat is often quite unsteady, a navigator often needs both arms and both legs to brace himself.

815. What does zenith mean? This is the spot in the heavens directly over the head of the observer.

816. What is the difference between latitude and longitude? Latitude is distance north or south of the equator. Longitude is distance east or west of Greenwich, England, which is at zero degrees longitude. Both latitude and longitude are expressed in degrees and fractions (minutes and seconds) of a circle.

817. How is the distance from a mark whose height is known determined with a sextant? The verticle angle from the horizon to the top of the object is measured with the sextant. This angle is then converted to minutes. Then apply the formula: $\dfrac{\text{height in feet} \times 0.57}{\text{angle (minutes)}}$ equals distance (nautical miles). For example: A lighthouse is recorded on the chart as 200 feet high. The sextant angle is one degree (60 minutes). Then $\dfrac{200 \times 0.57}{60}$ equals 1.9 nautical miles.

818. What difficulty does the navigator of a small boat encounter in taking sights? The navigator's height-of-eye above the water is very slight. If there is any sea running, he is always in danger of mistaking the top of a wave for the horizon. This will cause his sight to be quite inaccurate.

819. What is an octant? This is an early form of sextant. Octants were usually made of wood (ebony mostly). They were much larger than a sextant. They are no longer used for navigation but are collector's items.

820. What is Consolan? This is the name given a new method of navigation by use of a low-frequency radio receiver equipped with a beat frequency oscillator (BFO).

Developed during World War II by the Germans for air navigation under the name Soune, it was picked up and improved by the British under the name Consol. The United States system, which differs somewhat from the British, is called Consolan.

821. How does Consolan work? The Consolan station broadcasts its characteristic signals continuously. These signals consist of dots and dashes or dashes and dots. They are so beamed that the combination of dots and dashes (or dashes and dots) spans only a narrow sector from each station. By counting the dots and dashes and noting which is heard first, a navigator can determine in which sector he is located if he already has a fairly good dead reckoning position.

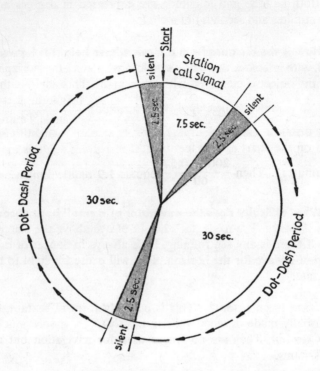

Nantucket and San Francisco Consolan stations transmit on 75-second operating cycle

822. How accurate is Consolan? It gives a more accurate position than a radio direction finder but is less accurate than loran. Daytime signals are accurate within 0.3 degrees (18′); night signals, 0.7 degrees (42′). Properly understood and used Consolan is the best electronic aid to navigation available to the small-boat owner. It is not, however, as accurate as a good three-star fix, taken with a sextant by a competent navigator. Consolan has an advantage over the sextant in that a reading can be taken regardless of weather conditions.

823. How is a Consolan bearing received? Using a direction finder (DF) receiver or a radio receiver with the beat frequency oscillator (BFO) turned on and the automatic volume control (AVC) turned off, a Consolan signal can be picked up.

824. Are Consolan signals audible for 360 degrees from the sending station? No, they are heard most clearly when the receiver is located on a bearing 90 degrees from an axis line drawn between the Consolan towers. Accuracy decreases gradually on both sides of this bearing. When the receiver's bearing is 20 degrees or less from the axis line, the signal is not reliable.

825. At what distance can U.S. Consolan signals be heard over water? From 50 to 1,000 or more miles. Closer than 50 miles, signals cannot be read.

826. How many Consolan stations are operated by the U.S. government? Only two at this writing. They are located at Nantucket, Massachusetts, on the East Coast and at San Francisco, California, on the West Coast.

827. What is the difference between British Consol and U.S. Consolan? The British use three towers, the U.S. only two at each Consolan station.

828. After a Consolan signal has been received is it necessary to make a correction before plotting the position on a mercator chart? Yes, it is necessary to use a conversion table which is contained in H.O. Publication, No. 117 (formerly No. 205).

829. What government publications are required for Consolan navigation? On the East Coast charts H.O. 1411 or H.O. 16,500; on the West Coast, H.O.-VC 70-4.

Also required are the Consolan tables contained in H.O. Publication No. 117 (formerly No. 205), "Radio Navigational Aids."

830. What are the principal characteristics of U.S. Consolan stations?

Name	Call Signal	Frequency (kc)	Power (kw)
Nantucket	TUK	194	2.5
San Francisco	SFI	192	7.2

831. Is Consolan suitable for use on small boats? Yes, it is practical on any boat big enough to carry a low frequency radio receiver and a Consolan chart.

832. What is loran? This is a new system of navigation in which Loran stations, operated by the government, spread an electronic line of position grid over a very wide area. A Loran receiver can pick up the signals and identify them in any weather. A navigator, by taking readings on two widely separated Loran stations, can pinpoint his position or, in navigator's language, get a fix.

Loran equipment is expensive and is not suitable for small boats, not only because the receiver is bulky but also because it consumes more current than is usually available except on large vessels.

833. What is radar? This is an electronic instrument that shows a "picture" of its immediate area in all directions, to a distance of two or three miles. The picture might be compared to a very poorly defined image seen occasionally on a television screen. By its means it is possible for a navigator to detect other boats, obstructions, etc., even in thick fog or at night. However, radar is expensive and requires the service of an experienced operator. It is not for small boats.

It is easy to spot a radar-equipped vessel by the continually rotating radar screen near the masthead. This picks up and transmits to the scope a picture of the surrounding area.

834. What is a radio direction finder (RDF)? This is an electronic device that enables a navigator to fix his position by taking bearings on two or more fixed radio beacons.

In addition, an RDF can be used to "home" on a single station located where the navigator wants to make an approach, such as a radio beacon at a harbor's entrance, a light vessel or Texas tower in a fairway.

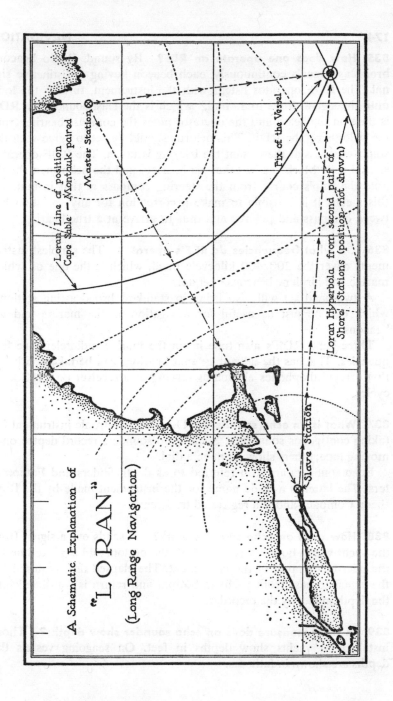

A Schematic Explanation of

"LORAN"

(Long Range Navigation)

Master Station

Loran Line of position
Cape Sable — Montauk paired

Fix of the Vessel

Loran Hyperbola from second pair of
Shore Stations (position not shown)

Slave Station

835. How does one operate an RDF? By sound. Radio beacons broadcast signals continuously, each beacon having a distinctive signal. The RDF operator listens with the instrument, turning the loop until the signal drops to a "null," which is the least sound. The RDF is then on the beam and the operator notes the compass bearing from the pelorus on the RDF. This pelorus should be set to agree with the ship's compass at the instant the bearing is taken. The RDF operator should call "Mark" as he takes his bearing, and the helmsman should note the ship's course from the steering compass at that instant. By this means it is possible to make a correction for any variation between compass and pelorus and thus to arrive at a true bearing.

836. On what frequencies do RDF's operate? The simplest instruments cover the 200/400 kilocycle band, which is the one on which marine and airplane beacons operate.

A two-band set will also bring in standard broadcasting stations, which can be just as useful for navigation as the marine and air beacons.

Three-band RDF's also tune in on the marine radiotelephone frequencies. This has the advantage that bearings can be taken on boats that carry radiophones as well as serving as a receiver on 2182 kilocycles.

837. What is an echo sounder? This is an electronic instrument for taking continuous soundings. Some echo sounders record depths on a moving tape; others show them on a dial.

Echo sounders are also referred to as depth finders and Fathometers. The latter is a trade name for the instrument made by the Raytheon Company and is a registered trademark.

838. How does an echo sounder work? It sends out a signal from the yacht which bounces (echoes) off the bottom and is picked up by the microphone part of the instrument. The elapsed time required for the signal to pass from yacht to bottom and return is translated into the depth in feet by the recorder.

839. In what measure does an echo sounder show depths? Those installed on yachts show depths in feet. On seagoing vessels the depths are shown in fathoms.

840. What is a lead? A lead (rhymes with bed) is a device for taking soundings. It is a heavy lead casting attached to a long line called a lead line. The line is marked so depths can be determined by observation of its markings when the lead is on the bottom of the water.

841. How heavy is a sounding lead? Sounding leads are available in several weights from two to sixteen pounds. The heaviest is called a deep-sea, or "dipsy," lead.

Blue pigeon was a nickname used by deep-water sailors for a deep-sea lead.

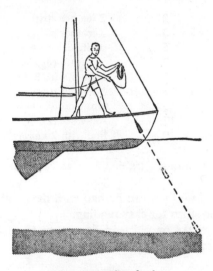

Using a sounding lead

842. What is meant by taking a sounding? The act of heaving the lead to the bottom to determine the depth at that point is called taking a sounding.

843. What does arming the lead mean? In the bottom of a sounding lead there is a shallow depression. This can be filled with tallow or grease to pick up a sample of the bottom for identification. This is called arming the lead.

844. How long is a lead line? For deep-sea use the conventional length is 20 fathoms (120 feet), but for yachts the line may be any convenient length, depending on the depth of water in which the yacht will be navigated.

Commercially, lead lines are available in 7, 10, 15, and 20 fathom lengths.

845. What are the traditional markings on a deep-sea sounding lead-line? The total length of the line is 20 fathoms (120 feet), which is marked as follows:

Fathoms	Marks
2	2 leather strips
3	3 leather strips
5	white cotton rag
7	red wool rag
10	leather with hole
13	3 leather strips
15	white cotton rag
17	red wool rag
20	line with 2 knots

The unmarked fathoms (which had to be estimated) were called "deeps."

Modern yacht lead lines can be had with the depths in plain figures printed on plastic strips for easy reading.

The peculiar marks on old lead lines were to enable the leadsman to determine soundings in the dark by feel.

XII. FLAGS, SIGNALS, AND SIGNALING

Introduction. Aside from either radio, voice, or Morse code, there are many other ways to communicate on the water. There are audible fog and passing signals to prevent collisions, flags to identify yacht clubs, boat owners, and the nationality of a yacht. International code flags also give meaning to individual letters of the alphabet, numbers and, by codes, a variety of special situations. Lights in various arrangements identify a boat, while running lights indicate its course. All of these put together enable yachtsmen to communicate swiftly and easily on the water. The sea has a language of its own, and the competent seaman learns to understand and use it.

846. What does one short blast on a signal horn indicate? A vessel in a meeting situation giving one short blast indicates that she intends to pass another portside to portside.

847. What do two short blasts on a signal horn indicate? A vessel in a meeting situation giving this signal indicates that she intends to pass another boat starboard to starboard.

848. What is the meaning of four short blasts on a signal horn? This indicates danger, that a signal is not understood or that a maneuver would be dangerous to carry out.

849. How is a passing signal answered? If the signal is understood and the maneuver can be executed without danger, it is proper to answer with the same signal as that given.

850. Where did yachting etiquette and flag routine originate? The origins of yachting etiquette and flag routines can be traced to Naval procedure. Modifications have been made to adapt to civilian usage, and time itself creates traditions, which governs all such ceremonial customs.

851. What authority determines the proper flags to be flown by yachts? Most clubs have a yacht routine that is followed by member

INLAND WATERS
FLAG ETIQUETTE
For Yachts in Commission and Manned

WHEN FLOWN	FLAG			TIME
	YACHT ENSIGN	Also When Under Power		
At Anchor				8 A.M. TO SUNSET
Under Way	Gaff			8 A.M. TO DARK
	CLUB BURGEE			
At Anchor				8 A.M. TO SUNSET
Under Way	Same as Above			8 A.M. TO DARK

					8 A.M. TO SUNSET
At Anchor	none				none
Under Way		SAME AS ABOVE			8 A.M. TO DARK

FLAG OFFICER'S FLAG

				DAY AND NIGHT
At Anchor				
Under Way	SAME AS ABOVE			

ALSO WHEN ABOARD ANOTHER MEMBER'S YACHT ON OFFICIAL BUSINESS

FOREIGN NATIONAL ENSIGN

When in Foreign Waters	At Starboard Spreader	If there is no spreader		8 A.M. TO SUNSET
At Anchor & Under Way				

NOTE: Custom varies among different clubs. In some, for example, the private signal displaces the club burgee at the truck of single-masted sailboats and the bow staff of mastless powerboats, when they are under way.

boat owners. Many clubs follow the routine of the North American Yacht Racing Union.

852. What flags are flown by a sloop at anchor or under power? The yacht ensign is flown from a staff at the stern. The yacht club burgee of the owner is flown at the truck (top) of the mainmast. If the owner is a yacht club officer, his official flag flies in place of the yacht club burgee.

853. What flags are flown by a two-masted yacht at anchor or under power? The same flags as on a sloop are flown, except that the private signal or officer's flag of the owner is carried at the head of the mizzen on a yawl or ketch. On a schooner the owner's private signal or house flag is carried at the head of the mainmast and the yacht club burgee in the same position on the foremast.

854. What flags does a sailboat carry when under sail but not racing? The same flags are flown as when at anchor except for the yacht ensign. On a sloop, a private signal is sometimes flown at the masthead in place of a club burgee. The private signal or the yacht ensign may occasionally be seen flying from the leech of a mainsail, and this is perfectly proper.

European yachts make it a practice to fly their ensigns at the taffrail staff even when under sail, but it is not customary in the United States.

855. What do the NAYRU racing rules say about flags that may be carried while racing? The owner's private signal may be carried on the leech of the mainsail (sloops) or at the mizzen truck (yawls and ketches). Also, the rules say that any wind indicator flown at the main masthead must be a solid-color flag or a feather. These are the only flags that may be carried while racing according to NAYRU rules.

856. What flags are flown by a yacht at anchor after sunset and before 8:00 A.M.? None need be flown. Sometimes, however, a yacht will fly a nighthawk (a long, narrow, blue pennant) at the main masthead.

857. Are officer's flags lowered at sunset? No, an officer's flag flies day and night except when racing. On a sloop it flies in place of the club burgee, and on a two-masted vessel in place of the private signal.

858. Are flags carried by a yacht under way at night? Yes. Normally the same flags that are carried in daylight hours are carried by a yacht under way after sunset.

859. What lights are shown at night by a yacht at anchor? On a yacht anchored in a channel a single white light is carried at or near the bow, some distance above the deck. This is called an anchor or riding light. In customary mooring areas, outside of regular channels, riding lights are usually dispensed with.

860. Do the rules on lights that must be carried by vessels under way between sunset and sunrise vary according to where you are? Yes, if you are under way in international waters you must carry the lights prescribed by International Rules. If you are afloat on inland waters, western rivers, or the Great Lakes you may show either the lights required under International Rules or the lights prescribed by the Motorboat Act of 1940. However, if you operate only on inland waters, you should be familiar with the additional requirements for stern lights, anchor lights, and other special lights under Inland, Western Rivers, and Great Lakes Rules.

861. Are there other requirements in some waters with regard to lights? Yes. If operating on inland waters under the jurisdiction of states or local authorities, skippers should make themselves familiar with applicable local regulations. These can vary considerably from place to place.

862. Is there a penalty for failure to comply with light regulations? Yes. Failure to display required lights may make a vessel liable to a $500 penalty.

863. What flags are carried by powerboats?   A powerboat either at anchor or under way flies the yacht club burgee of her owner at the bow, a private signal at the masthead (if she has one), and the yacht ensign at the stern.

864. May a national ensign ever be carried on yachts?   Yes. The national ensign may be displayed in place of the yacht ensign on documented yachts. However, this is rarely done.

865. Where is the yacht ensign carried under way by powerboats that have gaffs?   While under way a powerboat with a gaff on her mainmast flies the yacht ensign in this position. At anchor she carries the ensign on a stern staff like any other vessel.

866. What is a Union Jack?   This is a rectangular dark blue flag with 50 white stars, equal to the number of states of the Union.

867. When and where is the Union Jack flown?   The Union Jack is carried on the bow staff (jackstaff), of both sailing yachts and power yachts with more than one mast, between morning and evening colors while moored or at anchor, and only on Sundays, holidays, and dress-ship occasions.

868. What is a private signal?   A private signal is the personal flag of a yacht owner that can be of any design he chooses. Many are illustrated in color in Lloyd's Register of American Yachts. In some cases yacht club yearbooks also illustrate the flags of their members. Most private signals are in the form of swallowtails but may be any shape the owner prefers. Few are triangular. Private signals are also referred to as house flags. This name harks back to the days of clipper ships, whalers, and the packets which carried so many immigrants to this country in the early days. As these ships were usually owned by firms or, as they were also called, "houses," their identifying flags were called house flags. They were usually big rectangular flags with simple, easily-seen-at-a-distance designs. After all, the purpose of such a flag is for identification, so the simpler and bolder the design, the better it is. Some of the private signals shown in Lloyd's Register are laughable, as they would be impossible to identify at any distance at all.

869. What flag indicates that an owner is not aboard his boat?   A square blue flag flown from the starboard spreader of the mainmast indicates that the owner is absent.

870. What does a square blue flag with a white diagonal stripe carried at the starboard spreader indicate?   This is a guest flag and it indicates that there are guests of the owner aboard but that he himself is not present.

871. What does a rectangular white flag displayed at the starboard main spreader indicate?   This is the owner's meal flag and is displayed during the owner's meal hours between sunrise and sunset when a vessel is at anchor.

872. When cruising in foreign waters what additional flag is flown as a courtesy to the host country?   The national ensign of the country visited is displayed between morning and evening colors, at anchor or under way, at the bow staff of vessels without masts, at the starboard spreader of single-masted yachts, and at the starboard foremost spreader of yachts with two or more masts.

873. When a commodore or other flag officer is visiting another yacht, what flags are flown?   The flag officer's flag is flown at the truck of the highest mast on the vessel he is visiting. If one commodore is visiting another who happens to own a two-masted vessel, commodores' flags are flown at the trucks of both masts.

874. What size should the yacht ensign be?   The yacht ensign should be about one inch on the fly (length) for each foot of overall length of the vessel. The hoist of a yacht ensign is two-thirds the length of the fly.

875. What size should burgees, private signals, and officer's flags be?   These flags should be about one-half inch on the fly for each foot of height of the highest truck above the water on a sailboat. For a powerboat, the fly should equal about one-half inch for each foot of overall length. In both cases, the hoist is two thirds of the fly.

876. What size should a wind pennant be? A wind pennant should be about three quarters of an inch on the fly for each foot of height of the truck above the water. The hoist is normally one tenth of the fly.

This rule applies also to nighthawks.

877. On flags with one or more five-point stars, how should the stars be oriented? The star or stars should be displayed so that a single point points vertically upward. On flags where the stars are arranged in a circle, however, the axis of each star should radiate from the circle's center.

878. How many yacht club burgees may be carried at one time? No more than one yacht club burgee should be displayed on any vessel at one time.

879. When are flags half-masted? The ensign is half-masted only on occasions of national mourning. On Memorial Day the ensign is half-masted from 0800 to 1200. If displayed, the Union Jack is half-masted concurrently.

On the death of a yacht owner the burgee and private signal are half-masted on his boat.

When mourning the death of a member, only the club burgee is half-masted by other members' yachts at anchor and on the club flagstaff.

880. What is the procedure for bringing flags to half-mast? If not previously hoisted, flags are first hoisted to the truck and then lowered to half-mast.

In striking colors, flags are first hoisted to the truck from half-mast and then lowered.

881. What is the order of making colors? If possible, all flags are hoisted and lowered together.

When making colors short-handed, the ensign is hoisted first, followed in rapid order by the yacht club burgee and the private signal. These flags are lowered in inverse order.

Flags should be hoisted smartly but lowered more slowly and ceremoniously.

882. How should a club flagpole be designed? A club flagpole is often designed to resemble the farthest aft mast of a gaff-rigged vessel standing out to sea. It should be oriented and its flags should be flown accordingly.

The yacht ensign is flown at the gaff with this arrangement and the club burgee at the truck. If the flagstaff has no gaff, the yacht ensign is flown at the truck.

883. What is the proper way to call a launch? In most harbors, three blasts on a horn and the display of International Code flag "T" will summon a yacht club launch.

In harbors where there is more than one yacht club, each club should have a different horn signal to call its launch.

884. What is the proper fog signal for a vessel under way under power? One long blast on a horn every minute indicates a powered vessel under way in poor visibility.

885. What is the proper fog signal for a sailboat under way on starboard tack? One short blast every minute.

886. What is the proper fog signal for a sailboat under way on port tack? Two short blasts every minute.

887. What is the proper fog signal for an anchored boat? A short rapid bell ringing every minute.

888. How are the flags of the International Code used in signaling? The Oceanographic Office of the U.S. Navy publishes a book (H.O.87) in which are listed thousands of messages which can be sent by displaying one or more code flags on a single halyard. This is called a signal hoist. Flags are read from the top down.

Every well-found yacht should carry a set of Code signals and a copy of H.O.87.

889. How many flags make up the International Code of Signals? There are 26 letter flags, 10 numeral pennants, 3 repeaters, and a code or answering pennant—a total of 40 flags.

890. What are the names or designations of the individual International Code flags? So there can be no mistake when speaking of code flags, each one is given a distinctive name as follows:

A — Alfa	N — November
B — Bravo	O — Oscar
C — Charlie	P — Papa
D — Delta	Q — Quebec
E — Echo	R — Romeo
F — Foxtrot	S — Sierra
G — Golf	T — Tango
H — Hotel	U — Uniform
I — India	V — Victor
J — Juliet	W — Whisky
K — Kilo	X — X-ray
L — Lima	Y — Yankee
M — Mike	Z — Zulu

891. What does it mean to dress ship? A yacht with a hoist of signal flags reaching from her bow to her masthead and back down to her stern is said to be dressed.

There is no set order in which the signal flags must be hoisted, but various arrangements to create the most colorful or most orderly display have been suggested.

892. During dress-ship do the normal flags remain in place? Yes, and they are never mixed with the code flags.

893. What is Morse code? This is an international signal system employing dots and dashes to represent the letters of the alphabet, as follows:

A	•—	didah'	J	•———	didah'dah'dah'
B	—•••	dah'dididit	K	—•—	dah'didah'
C	—•—•	dah'didah'dit	L	•—••	didah'didit
D	—••	dah'didit	M	——	dah'dah'
E	•	dit	N	—•	dah'dit
F	••—•	dididah'dit	O	———	dah'dah'dah'
G	——•	dah'dah'dit	P	•——•	didah'dah'dit
H	••••	didididit	Q	———•—	dah'dah'didah'
I	••	didit	R	•—•	didah'dit

S	• • •	dididit	W	• — —	didah'dah'
T	—	dah	X	— • • —	dah'dididah'
U	• • —	dididah'	Y	— • — —	dah'didah'dah'
V	• • • —	didididah'	Z	— — • •	dah'dah'didit

Numbers

1	• — — — —	didah'dah'dah'dah'
2	• • — — —	dididah'dah'dah'
3	• • • — —	didididah'dah'
4	• • • • —	dididididah'
5	• • • • •	dididididit
6	— • • • •	dah'dididit
7	— — • • •	dah'dah'dididit
8	— — — • •	dah'dah'dah'didit
9	— — — — •	dah'dah'dah'dah'dit
0	— — — — —	dah'dah'dah'dah'dah'

894. What is the Coastal Warning System? The U.S. Weather Bureau employs a system for wind and weather warning signals at stations along all seacoasts, on the Great Lakes, the Hawaiian Islands, and Puerto Rico.

895. What are the small-craft warning signals? One red pennant displayed in daylight hours, and a red over a white light at night, indicate that winds up to 33 knots and/or sea conditions dangerous to the operations of small craft are forecast for the area.

896. What are the gale warning signals? Two red pennants by day and a white over a red light at night, mean that 34–47 knot winds are forecast for the area.

897. What are the whole gale warning signals? A single square red flag with a square black center by day, and two red lights at night, indicate that 48–63 knot winds are forecast for the area.

898. What is the Coastal Warning Display System signal for a hurricane warning? Two square red flags with square black centers by day, and a white light between two red lights, vertically displayed, at night, indicate that winds of 64 knots and above may be expected in the area.

899. What is meant by "Mayday"?   This is the international designation for a distress signal broadcast by radiotelephone. It is the equivalent of SOS in Morse code. The person giving such a call should loudly call the word "Mayday" into the phone several times to warn all listeners that the following message is a call for help.

900. How should a "Mayday" call be made?   Repeat the word "Mayday" three times; give the name of the boat, its exact position as accurately as possible, state the nature of the emergency, and, finally, tell what assistance is required.

After the call has been acknowledged, further details can be given —such as the color and description of your boat and any other pertinent information.

901. On what radio frequency is the "Mayday" signal broadcast? The international distress frequency is 2182 kilocycles.

902. If a "Mayday" signal is heard what is the proper procedure?   Any person hearing a "Mayday" call should immediately cease any message he may be sending to clear the air for the distress call. He should listen in and try to find out the name of the boat in distress, her location, and the nature of the distress.

If near enough to be of assistance he should proceed at full speed to the rescue. At the same time he should notify the caller that he is coming and when he expects to arrive.

903. What signal is used to indicate that an emergency may be developing?   If an emergency is developing on board your boat, or if you see another boat which appears to be getting into trouble, the signal to send by radiophone is the word "Pan" repeated three times. When the call is acknowledged state the situation clearly and briefly.

904. What is a "safety" message?   This is notification of approaching trouble, such as a storm warning or the existence of an uncharted navigation hazard. Such a message should be preceded by the word "security" repeated three times.

905. What does "roger" mean?   The reply "roger" means "received and understood."

906. What does the word "Conelrad" mean? This is an emergency signal sent out by Civil Defense to warn of an impending enemy attack.

907. Besides a radiophone, what means of signaling for help is available to the boatman? Perhaps the oldest call for help is to display the yacht ensign or the national flag upside down.

Firing of flares or rockets at night or orange smoke signals by day is a well-recognized call for help.

Hoisting the International Code signals DZ means "I need immediate assistance"; the hoist NC means "I am in distress and need immediate assistance."

And everyone knows what SOS stands for. This signal can also be wigwagged or sent in Morse code.

Blowing a horn or ringing a bell continuously is a recognized call for help and, if a gun is carried aboard, firing it at one-minute intervals to attract attention is a distress signal.

At night or by day, Morse code signals can be sent with a flashlight.

Facing a possible source of help and raising the arms from the side of the legs to overhead, in a radial motion, rapidly, is an international distress signal.

908. What kind of pyrotechnics are used in distress signaling? There are available flares, rockets of various kinds and smoke signals. The former are primarily for night use, while smoke is more effective by day.

Flares and rockets can be of various colors. There is a parachute flare which remains aloft for some time, floating slowly down, supported by its tiny parachute.

These signals are made so they can be hand-held, and there are also shells for use with a Verey pistol.

909. What is a Verey pistol? This is a hand-held firearm which is used to discharge signal rockets into the air. Primarily it is a distress signal. Verey pistols come in two sizes: the smaller has a bore or gauge of 0.98 inch (25 mm.). The larger takes a shell 1.45 inches (37 mm.) in diameter.

XIII. RACING

Introduction. Almost all types of boats, both power and sail, are raced in many different kinds of competition. Generally speaking, the rewards for winning are trophies. Only in hydroplane and offshore powerboat racing are there cash prizes. Another type of competition for powerboats is the predicted log contest, which is strictly amateur.

Racing for sailboats can be broken down into two categories—"around the buoys" for all types of boats and distance, or port-to-port racing for the cruising types. The latter is normally done on a handicap and corrected time basis, whereas small boats race boat-for-boat by individual classes, in which case the boat with the best elapsed time wins. When cruising boats race around the buoys, it is on a handicap basis just as in distance racing.

910. What national organization governs sailboat racing in this country? The North American Yacht Racing Union, located at 37 West 44th Street, New York, N. Y., 10036. Their racing rules and regulations are used practically exclusively in this hemisphere. The NAYRU, in turn, belongs to the International Yacht Racing Union (IYRU), which governs sailing throughout the world.

911. Who may belong to the NAYRU? Associations of yacht clubs, yacht clubs, and individuals who are members of recognized yacht clubs.

912. How many associations of yacht clubs belong to the NAYRU? In 1965 there were 33 associations of yacht clubs which were members of the NAYRU. They included clubs in every yachting center in the United States and Canada.

913. When did sailing become an Olympic sport. In 1896.

914. What classes are used in the Olympics? This can vary each Olympic year. In 1960, 1964, and 1968 the 5.5-Meter, Dragon, Star, Flying Dutchman, and Finn Classes took part.

915. What is the oldest Olympic class?   The Star Class.

916. In what classes have Olympic Gold Medals in sailing been won for the United States?

> *5.5-Meter Class*
>
> > 1952—Dr. Britton Chance
> > 1960—George O'Day
>
> *Star Class*
>
> > 1932—Gilbert Gray
> > 1948—Hilary Smart
> > 1956—Herbert Williams

917. What has been the best overall showing by a United States sailing team in Olympic competition?   In the 1964 Tokyo Olympics, even though no Gold Medals were won by the United States representatives, every team member won a medal. In bringing home two Silver and three Bronze Medals, the team set a new high for overall performance. Never before had a country placed in every Olympic sailing class in the same year.

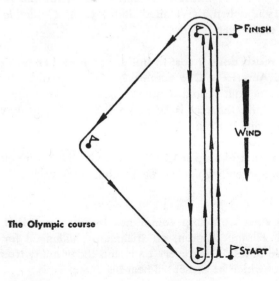

The Olympic course

918. What racing course is used most frequently in international competition?   The Olympic course.

919. What is an Olympic course?   It consists of six legs: three to windward, two reaches, and a run.

920. When was the Olympic course first used in America's Cup competition?   During 1964 in the races between the United States yacht *Constellation* and *Sovereign,* the British challenger.

921. Does "12-Meter" apply to any particular dimension of the America's Cup yachts?   No. The term 12-Meter is simply the maximum quotient that a formula, taking into account such factors as sail area, overall length, beam and draft, must not exceed.

922. What are the approximate dimensions of a 12-Meter yacht?
Length overall: 69 feet
Length on the waterline: 46 feet
Beam: 12 feet
Sail area: 1850 square feet

923. When were 12-Meter boats first used in races for the America's Cup?   In 1958 when the United States yacht *Columbia* defeated the British challenger *Sceptre.*

924. About how much does it cost to build, equip and campaign a 12-Meter for one America's Cup summer?   The sum of $600,000 is a rough approximation. About a quarter of this amount goes toward building the hull, the rest is spent on sails, spars, gear of all kinds, maintenance, and berthing the crew.

925. How many men make up a 12-Meter crew?   There are eleven men on a 12-Meter crew, which is the maximum number allowed under the rules.

926. Why is the America's Cup sometimes incorrectly called the Lipton Cup?   Sir Thomas Lipton, an Irishman, challenged for the America's Cup five times, losing every time, and today many trophies in the United States which he presented bear his name.

927. When was Sir Thomas Lipton's final challenge for the America's Cup?   In 1930 Sir Thomas sent over *Shamrock V* in his last challenge for the Cup.

928. During what years were the huge J-Class sloops used for competition in the America's Cup races?   In the years 1930, 1934, and 1937 these huge craft, over twice as large as a 12-Meter, were the America's Cup boats. They were required to reach the place of challenge on their own bottoms, which meant that the English challengers were at the considerable disadvantage of having to be capable of a trans-Atlantic passage.

929. Of what material are the 12-Meters built?   They are built of wood. The J boats, however, were normally built of steel or bronze.

930. Who has sailed more successful United States Cup defenders than any other man?   Harold S. Vanderbilt sailed three—*Enterprise,* 1930; *Rainbow,* 1934; and *Ranger,* 1937.

931. In what year were the Cup races first sailed off Newport, Rhode Island?   In 1930.

932. Where were America's Cup races sailed prior to 1930?   The early races were sailed off Sandy Hook, outside New York Harbor.

933. What nations other than England have challenged for the cup?   Canada—1876, *Countess of Dufferin,* and 1881, *Atalanta.*
Australia—1962, *Gretel,* and 1967.

934. What is the Mallory Cup?   This is the trophy for the North American men's sailing championship competition which has been held annually since 1952. The skipper must be over eighteen years of age, but there is no restriction on the ages or sex of participant crew members.

935. What is the Mrs. Charles Francis Adams Trophy?   This is the prize for an annual competition for the women's national sailing championship which has been raced for since 1924.

936. What is the Sears Cup?   This is the trophy representing the North American junior sailing championship. Originally placed in competition only for Massachusetts Bay yacht club juniors in 1921, it first was expanded to include Long Island Sound a year later, and became national in 1931.

937. What is the O'Day Trophy?   This is a trophy representing the North American singlehanded sailing championship. It has been in competition since 1962.

938. How is a decision reached on where to hold the National Sailing Championships each year?   The four championships are rotated among the eight areas into which the 33 NAYRU member associations of yacht clubs are grouped.

939. How many elimination series must a contestant go through to reach a National Sailing Championship?   Normally there are four. First, the individual must be chosen to represent his yacht club. He will then have to win or place high (it varies) in a series in his local area, which is a small part of one of 33 NAYRU associations of yacht clubs. He will then have to win the association championship and, finally, one of eight area titles. (The 33 member associations of yacht clubs are combined into eight areas.)

940. What is the best known and most important ocean race in U.S. Atlantic Coast waters?   The biennial race from Newport, Rhode Island, to Bermuda, sponsored by the Cruising Club of America and the Royal Bermuda Yacht Club. It is 635 miles in length and open only to yachts that are owned by CCA or RBYC members and those which are invited to take part. It was first sailed in 1906 and has been on a biennial basis since 1924 (except for 1940–1944).

941. What is the most important ocean race on the West Coast?   The biennial race from Los Angeles, California, to Diamond Head in Honolulu. This race is 2,225 nautical miles in length and is often called the Transpac or The Honolulu Race. It is sponsored by the Transpacific YC, the first race having been sailed in 1906, and is now run in odd years.

942. What are some of the other important, regularly scheduled, distance or ocean races around the world?

(1) The Fastnet Race is 600 miles long, and sailed, in England, every other year.

(2) The Sidney–Hobart Race, 630 miles long, and sailed yearly.

(3) The Buenos Aires–Rio de Janeiro Race, 1,200 miles long, and sailed every third year.

943. Is there any distance racing on the Great Lakes? Every year there are races from Chicago and Port Huron, near Detroit, to Mackinac Island. In addition, there are a number of shorter races to and from various other ports. The two mentioned are the most important, however.

944. In a distance race what happens at night? Does the entire crew stay up or sleep at the same time? No. There is a watch system established so that approximately half the crew is on deck at any given time. The skipper, navigator, and cook may not stand watches.

945. What is the MORC? MORC stands for Midget Ocean Racing Club, a national organization with many local racing fleets which has a measurement rating rule and standard set of conditions for distance racing of cruising auxiliaries under 30 feet in overall length. The mailing address of their headquarters is Box 4092, Grand Central Station, New York, N.Y. 10017.

946. What is the One-of-a-Kind Regatta? This is an event for racing classes and is held every few years, under the auspices of *Yachting* magazine, when the time seems appropriate. Boats race in four or five classes according to type. One boat only from each class may participate. Regattas have been held in several localities.

947. What determines the top speed that a displacement-type sailboat can achieve? The waterline length of the hull determines the maximum speed that a displacement sailboat can go through the water. By various experiments, it has been found that this function is equal to about 1.34 times the square root of the waterline length. Thus a boat that is 25 feet l.w.l. can theoretically sail no faster than 6.7

knots ($\sqrt{25} \times 1.34 = 6.7$). This is usually referred to as "hull speed."

948. What factors determine the top speeds of planing-type hulls? The factors involved include the hull's displacement at top speed, skin friction and wave-making resistance, and engine and propeller efficiency. The latter, of course, only applies to powerboats. In the case of sailboats, wind speed will be an important factor.

949. Where may a copy of the "Official Sailboat Racing Rules" be obtained? From the Corresponding Secretary, North American Yacht Racing Union, 37 West 44th Street, New York, N.Y. 10036.

950. What is a good source of information on running sailboat races? The North American Yacht Racing Union's "Race Committee Handbook" covers a variety of subjects on recommended procedure for conducting yacht races. It is available from the NAYRU for $1.50.

951. In a series of races how is a boat scored? In this country, one point is usually given for starting, one for finishing, and one for each boat beaten. An extra quarter of a point is awarded for finishing first.

952. Why is Olympic scoring not used exclusively in this country? Because the Olympic ideal places a tremendous premium on winning rather than consistently placing high, which many people feel is a more desirable ability.

953. How is a professional yachtsman defined? A professional is defined as one who works full-time aboard a yacht as a means of making a livelihood, as distinguished from an amateur who takes part only as a pastime, or a student, or other junior, who may work for pay during a vacation. People who gain their living by serving the needs of boat owners (yacht designers, builders, sailmakers, etc.) are not considered professionals.

954. Are professionals prohibited by the rules from handling a boat during a race? The NAYRU racing rules state that a paid hand shall not steer a yacht of less than 32 feet waterline length. Class rules and race circulars also often state the numbers and positions that must be filled by amateurs.

955. What is a Predicted Log Contest? This is a contest for powerboats in which the winner is that yacht which has the lowest percentage of error over a specified course, in relation to what was predicted by her skipper before the start.

956. How are Predicted Log Contests run? This is a piloting contest. The committee furnishes only a minimum of piloting information, a list of checkpoints, and the finish time. Skippers receive rules and log sheets well in advance of the contest. They must predict their starting time and the times of passing official checkpoints (or elapsed time for each leg) and return the written log to the committee before the start. The boat finishing with the minimum error is the winner. High speed is not a factor.

957. What rules apply at the start of a Predicted Log Contest? The official starting time for each boat is the predicted time recorded in the boat's log before the start. No starting error is charged, but a contestant must start within two minutes of the predicted time or risk disqualification.

958. Is there a minimum average speed that must be maintained during a Predicted Log Contest? This may vary according to the conditions of the race, but generally a minimum of six knots is prescribed.

959. In a Predicted Log Contest, is it permissible to change speed? Yes. R.p.m. settings may be changed by the skipper at any time and need not be officially recorded.

960. In a Predicted Log Contest how must the boat be steered? The start and all control and intermediate points must be passed within 200 feet and the finish within 500 feet. For reasons of safety these distances may be increased.

Major deviations from the direct line course between control and intermediate check points are not permitted except for reasons of safety. Failure to adhere to this rule is grounds for disqualification.

961. May a contestant use radar or radio direction-finding equipment during a predicted Log Contest? A contestant may use this equipment to plot his position only in the case of seriously impaired visibility.

962. What information is not available to the skipper during a Predicted Log Contest? Except at the start, information that would give the time of day, elapsed time, speed through the water or over the ground, and distance traveled is not available to anyone but the observer during a Predicted Log Contest.

963. In a Predicted Log Contest what are the duties of the observer? During a contest no person aboard a competing yacht, except the observer, has access to the timepieces, logs, or speedometers. These are in the custody of the observer, and he is responsible for checking the actual times that control points are passed. After finishing, the observer also often computes the percentage error for his vessel and passes this information to the committee.

964. What organization governs practically all powerboat racing in this country? The American Power Boat Association governs the racing of everything from hydroplanes to offshore cruisers, including Predicted Log Contests. The address of the APBA is: 2534 St. Aubin Street, Detroit, Michigan 48207.

965. What function does the APBA perform? The APBA sanctions events, promulgates rules, and validates records.

966. Of what larger organization is the APBA a member? The APBA belongs to, and is the United States authority of, the Union of International Motorboating.

967. Who approves world records in powerboat racing? The aforementioned Union of International Motorboating.

968. Can plans for inboard hydroplanes be bought? Generally speaking, designers of inboard hydroplanes are also the builders and do not sell their plans to be built by others.

969. Can plans for outboard hydroplanes be bought? Yes. Several designers have stock plans available. Their names are available from APBA.

XIV. WATER SKIING AND TRAILERS

Introduction. One of the most popular water sports that is a direct outgrowth of the boating boom is water skiing. It is an easy sport to learn and one that can be very enjoyable. It is important before attempting water skiing to learn the basic safety rules, signals, and boat-handling techniques. It is also important for yachtsmen operating boats in the vicinity of water skiing to understand what is going on and what to look for.

One thing that has done a great deal to further interest in water skiing (and small boat sailing as well) is the trailer. People living far from water have found it possible to take their boats long distances in relative convenience with the development of specially designed and efficient trailers. In this fashion many more people are within reach of these water sports. Here also we present some of the rudiments of trailer handling on the highway and some helpful tips on launching and recovering.

970. What is the first essential of a properly equipped towboat for water skiing? A properly equipped towboat must have remote control steering and a wheel. Direct steering from the stern of a boat is dangerous and ill-advised.

971. How should a towline be attached to a boat for water skiing? The towline should be attached so that the pull is absorbed throughout the hull. The weight and leverage of a skier are sufficient to capsize a boat if pull is exerted on only one side.

972. What are some of the methods of attaching a towline to a water skiing boat? A strong eye bolt through the center of the transom is effective, as is a bracket attached to the lower unit of the outboard motor. If two eye bolts are installed on either side of the transom, a strong yoke between them is also effective. Pylons, made especially for towing, installed around the motor are probably best of all. They are usually mounted on the gunwales and braced to the transom.

973. Should a ski towboat have more than one person aboard when in operation? Yes, always. An observer is essential to keep watch and aid with fallen skiers.

974. What horsepower outboard motor will be required to pull one skier? With a driver and an observer in the boat, at least a 25-horsepower engine will be required to pull one skier. More power will be necessary if more than one skier at a time is to be pulled or if more passengers are to be carried.

975. What design characteristic is particularly desirable for a ski towboat? Wide beam in a ski towboat is very advantageous to stability in cornering.

976. What equipment should a ski towboat carry? Aside from the usual Coast Guard requirements, the well-equipped ski towboat should have a boarding ladder to aid fallen skiers and a large rear-view mirror so that the driver can observe what is going on astern without turning his head or having to rely on what the observer tells him.

977. What is the proper signal for the skier to give the driver in starting? The proper starting signal for a skier to indicate his readiness is "Hit it." "Go" sounds too much like "No."

978. How fast should a beginner be towed? A beginning skier will find that 15–18 m.p.h. is all he can handle. Speed should be just enough so that his skis will plane cleanly.

979. How should throttle adjustments be made by the driver? Throttle adjustments should be made slowly and evenly. Jerky throttle adjustments cause uneven slack in the towline, which is difficult for the skier to handle.

980. When returning to a fallen skier, what is the first thing to remember? Shut off the motor before you get too close. That propeller is dangerous.

981. What is the proper way to approach a fallen skier? When returning to a fallen skier always keep him on the driver's side so that he can be easily seen. If the approach is made with the boat heading into the wind there will be little chance of getting too close.

982. If a skier is outside the wake of the towboat, which way should the boat be turned? When cornering, a boat should always be turned in the direction opposite to the side on which the skier is located. Never turn into the skier—the jolt that comes when tension returns to the towline can capsize a boat or cause injury to the skier. If you must turn into the skier, chop the throttle and dunk him rather than risk an accident.

983. What is the proper pattern for returning a skier to shore? An in-and-out approach avoids running the boat parallel to the shoreline—an action which might disturb others.

984. What is an enjoyable speed for an experienced water skier? Normally 22–28 m.p.h. is enough for anybody. Speeds in excess of 30 m.p.h. are for experts only. Falls at such speeds are hard and can be dangerous.

985. What are ideal water skiing conditions? A straight path and minimum wake interference from other boats are highly desirable. There should be room enough to make turns away from shore to avoid disturbing others. If you stay in a constant pattern, other boatmen will see it and try to avoid the area.

986. What is the minimum safe depth for water skiing? Most experts agree that water should be at least four feet deep for safe water skiing.

987. If more than one skier is being pulled by the same boat at one time, how long should the tow ropes be? All tow ropes in this situation should be the same length.

988. What is skiing with one ski called? This is called slalom and is for more advanced water skiers.

989. What action is necessary on the part of a driver when his skier tries slalom for the first time? The driver should maintain a straight path to allow his skier to get the feel of the new technique. Slightly more speed will probably be required to compensate for the smaller skiing surface.

990. What is best for a water ski towline? The standard length of a towline is 70 feet with an additional 5 feet for the detachable handles. The most popular towline is ¼ inch polypropelene. This rope is brightly colored and floats, so that it can easily be seen in the water.

991. Where may instructional information on water skiing be obtained? Many booklets are available from the American Water Ski Association, Winter Haven, Florida.

992. What is the common water skiing hand signal given by a skier after a fall? Both hands clasped overhead indicates to the towboat that the skier is OK and in no danger.

993. What signals does a skier give to the towboat when he wants to go faster?
(1) Palm up—moved in upward direction.
(2) Thumb up—motion upward.
(3) Nod head.

994. What signals does a skier give to his towboat when he want go slower?
(1) Palm down—moved in a downward direction.
(2) Thumb down—motion downward.
(3) Shake head as if to say "No."

995. How does a skier indicate to the driver the exact speed he desires? The skier puts up the number of fingers for the speed he wants in two separate motions. Shouting can never be heard.

996. How does a skier indicate that he is satisfied with towboat speed as is? He makes an "OK" signal by forming an "O" with thumb and forefinger.

997. How does a skier indicate he wishes to turn? With his palm in a vertical position, he makes a curving motion with his hand in the direction he wishes to turn.

998. How does a skier indicate that he wishes to stop? Like a policeman directing traffic, he puts his hand up with fingers outstretched and together.

999. How does a water skier indicate to the towboat that he wishes the motor shut off? By running a finger across his throat in a cutting motion, the skier will get his message to an understanding driver.

1000. What is the most important consideration in selecting a trailer? Make sure that the trailer is long enough and of sufficient load capacity to handle the boat to be trailed.

1001. What should be remembered if the boat to be trailed has an engine? You will want to be sure that there is adequate support near the rear of the trailer where this considerable weight is concentrated.

1002. Why is it important to allow extra distance to stop when towing at trailer behind a car? The added weight of the trailer greatly increases the distance required to stop.

1003. What items should receive particular attention on a trailer rig? When driving any distance the hitch and safety chain should be inspected periodically to make sure they are functioning properly.

1004. On a long trailer trip what spare equipment should be carried? Here is a suggested list: spare wheel with tire, trailer jack, extra securing lines, spare wheel bearings, extra bearing grease, spare winch line.

1005. How do you back a trailer to the left? To the right? To back a trailer to the left, turn the steering wheel of the car to the right. To back to the right, turn your wheel to the left.

1006. What should be remembered in approaching a curve in the road when towing a trailer?   The trailer will make a shorter arc than the tires of the car. To avoid the possibility of the trailer tires leaving the road, take the curve as wide as is reasonably possible.

1007. Why is it important to make sure that trailer tires are inflated at manufacturer-recommended pressures?   Under-inflation causes excessive tire wear, which may cause a blowout.

1008. What is a trailer parking jack?   Located at the coupler end of the trailer, a parking jack keeps the trailer level when not attached to a car hitch, and facilities manual maneuvering of the rig.

1009. What is the proper manner of launching a boat from a boat trailer?   Back the trailer to within a few feet of the water's edge. Remove all tie-downs. Back the trailer to the edge of the water. Slowly push or allow the boat to slide off the trailer into the water.

1010. What is the proper manner of retrieving a boat from the water onto a trailer?   Reverse the launching procedure and make sure the boat rides up the rollers of the trailer correctly so as to protect the underbody from damage. Be sure that everything is secure before driving off.

1011. Why is it a good idea to keep a trailer axle dry?   A hot bearing from driving at highway speeds that is dunked in cold water is very apt to crack.

1012. What else happens when hot wheels are dunked in cold water?   As the wheels become hot while driving, the air inside the hubs expands. When they are suddenly cooled, the air contracts and water is sucked right past the grease seals and into the bearings. If the trailer must get wet to launch the boat, at least give the wheels a chance to cool.

1013. What should be done immediately after a trailer has been immersed in salt water?   It should be rinsed off with fresh water to minimize the potential effects of corrosion.

1014. Can a trailer have a power winch?   Yes. A power winch can be run off the car's electrical system.

1015. If a trailer is to be inactive for a long time, what should be done?   Remove the outboard motor if there is one. Loosen tie-downs. Block under axles to lift wheels clear of ground. Protect boat with ventilated cover if stored outside, and raise forward end of trailer so that water can run off.

INDEX

References are to question numbers

NOTES

NOTES

NOTES

NOTES

NOTES

NOTES

NOTES

NOTES

NOTES

NOTES